THE NEXT-GEN INFORMATION SECURITY PROFESSIONAL

VINCENT VAN DIJK

Colofon

ISBN:	9789083490960
Publisher:	Vincent van Dijk Publications
Edition:	1st edition
Editor:	Margaret Sarsfield
Design and DTP:	Astrid Honcoop
Cover design:	Astrid Honcoop
Writing coach:	Perdiep Ramesar

FOREWORD BY PROF. DR. YURI BOBBERT

Information security has progressed from a predominantly technical safeguard to a central component of organizational governance, strategy, and value creation. Rather than asking whether security is necessary, organizations must confront a more nuanced question:

How can security capabilities be designed, built, and operated to strengthen the organization and its performance reliably?

This book is meant to help in that transition. It shows you how to treat cybersecurity not as an isolated technical domain, but as a socio-technical discipline spanning leadership, architecture, behavior, and economics.

Several emerging movements underpin this reframing.

FROM COST CENTER TO RETURN ON SECURITY INVESTMENT

First, cybersecurity is increasingly evaluated through the lens of Return on Security Investment (RoSI). Security initiatives are no longer justified solely by reference to abstract threats or regulatory expectations. Boards and executive teams expect a clear articulation of:

- how specific controls reduce defined risks,
- how those reductions translate into avoided losses and preserved opportunities, and
- how security spending compares with alternative uses of capital.

The book equips you with ideas and relatable stories that allow security professionals to quantify, compare, and communicate the impact of their interventions in terms that resonate with finance, strategy, and operations.

CYBER RISK QUANTIFICATION AS DECISION SUPPORT

Closely connected to RoSI is the maturation of cyber risk quantification. Moving beyond qualitative "red–amber–green" heatmaps, organizations are beginning to adopt methods that estimate risk in financial and probabilistic terms.

When done well, cyber risk quantification enables:

- transparent justification of investments and trade-offs,
- prioritization of initiatives based on marginal risk reduction, and
- alignment of security posture with the organization's broader risk appetite.

This bookshows how important it is to view information security from a business perspective. Becoming proficient in risk helps you to convince stakeholders and drive impact.

THE CHIEF SECURITY ORCHESTRATOR

A second movement is the emergence of what can be termed the Chief Security Orchestrator. Traditional models of security leadership focused on ownership of specific domains—network, application, compliance, identity. In modern, highly interconnected enterprises, such fragmentation is no longer tenable.

The Chief Security Orchestrator is characterized less by direct control over every security function and more by the ability to:

- integrate policies, processes, and technologies into a coherent operating model,
- mediate between technical specialists and business leadership, and
- convene cross-functional collaboration across IT, risk, legal, HR, and line management.

The chapters in this book collectively reinforce this orchestration role. The book provides frameworks and examples that help you understand how diverse security activities can be aligned into a single, adaptive capability.

BUSINESS MODEL CANVAS AS A CROSS-SILO ENABLER

An essential and future-oriented development is the use of the Business Model Canvas (and related visual strategy tools) to bridge silos. By mapping value propositions, customer segments, key activities, resources, and partners, the Business Model Canvas makes visible the organizational context in which security must operate.

When security professionals work with such canvases, several benefits emerge:

- shared understanding between security, business, and technology stakeholders;
- explicit identification of where security risks concentrate within value creation mechanisms;
- more constructive dialogue about trade-offs between protection, usability, innovation, and speed.

The Risk Model Canvas chapter shows how the security profession can appropriate such tools as practical instruments for cross-silo collaboration, strategic alignment, and co-design of secure business models.

AI IN CYBERSECURITY: CAPABILITY AND EXPOSURE

Third, artificial intelligence (AI) is reshaping both the means and the ends of cybersecurity. On the defensive side, AI augments human capability in anomaly detection, threat hunting, incident triage, and simulation. On the offensive side, adversaries exploit AI for scalable social engineering, automated exploitation, and continuous reconnaissance.

The implication is not simply that "AI changes everything," but that security professionals must develop a nuanced literacy in:

- how new AI risks impact the business.
- how to deal with new technology and understand the underlying principles.
- the governance mechanisms required to keep AI-assisted decisions transparent, ethical, and contestable.

The examples and principles in this book contribute to that literacy. It treats AI as a component within a larger security architecture—subject to design, control, and oversight.

A PROFESSION THAT MUST CONTINUOUSLY LEARN

Across these developments runs a constant theme: cybersecurity is fundamentally a human profession embedded in organizations. Frameworks, metrics, and technologies are essential, but they do not replace professional judgment, ethical reflection, or the capacity to learn from incidents and near misses.

The most significant risk many organizations face is not the absence of a specific tool, but the presence of a workforce that is:

- insufficient proffesional skills,
- poorly integrated into decision-making processes, or
- unable to adapt to the pace of technological and regulatory change.

This book therefore, does more than present concepts; it supports professionalization. It underscores the need for continuous training, education, and development at all levels—from aspiring analysts to senior leaders. It encourages you to see yourself not merely as an operator of tools or guardian of compliance, but as contributor to an organization's mission.

Taken together, the perspectives in this volume help readers:

- frame cybersecurity in economic and strategic terms,
- adopt an orchestration mindset that transcends traditional silos,
- leverage tools like the Business Model Canvas to engage constructively with the business,
- critically integrate, understand the core princples of new developments like AI and their impact on information security,
- recognize continuous learning as a non-negotiable pillars of effective security.

For organizations, this book offers a structured lens through which to design and mature their security capabilities. For practitioners, it provides a roadmap for developing the knowledge, skills, and attitudes required in a profession that must remain perpetually in motion.

It is in that spirit of rigorous, future-oriented, and practice-relevant cyber-security that I commend this book to you.

Prof. Dr. Yuri Bobbert
Professor at Antwerp Management School

TABLE OF CONTENTS

INTRODUCTION

I didn't start out in cybersecurity. My background was in software engineering, and over time I began specializing in data science. In 2018, I scored an internship as a data scientist, but it came with an unexpected opportunity: a summer job as a security scientist.

This was my manager's idea, and the rationale was simple: Understand cybersecurity first, so I'd be more effective later. The only problem? I knew almost nothing about cybersecurity.

Sure, I'd "hacked" before—mostly cheating in online games or tinkering with anti-cheat systems when I hosted my own servers. But that was a far cry from real security work.

In the months before the summer job, I had to learn fast. I approached it like an engineer: I devoured books on cybersecurity—how hacking works, the tools hackers use, and the techniques behind attacks. By the time summer arrived, I was nervous, but ready.

Or so I thought.

I'd been on the job one day when I was called into a meeting with a senior security consultant. His opening question:

"Can we use machine learning in cybersecurity?"

I didn't know for sure, but I answered honestly: "I'm not sure, but I know where to look. I know we can do it. We can use machine learning to detect people behaving anomalously, then use other models to see if that behavior is also malicious."

His eyes lit up. I went on, brainstorming possibilities aloud until he was called away, cutting our conversation short. I never really spoke to him again; he was always busy with clients and, soon after, he moved on from the company. But he must have told others about me, because I soon found myself the go-to guy for machine learning questions. He'd come away from our brief discussion with the idea that I was a man with answers.

How had that happened?

It wasn't the quality of my ideas; anyone who did understand them likely would have known they were impractical or wrong.

It wasn't my background; I barely knew anything about machine learning—just a few techniques.

Over time, I realized it must have been those six words: "I know we can do it." More than expertise or even being right, it was my attitude that made the difference.

In 1916, psychologist Edward Thorndike wrote: "The response a pupil makes to any situation is caused in large measure by his attitude or mind-set." He was among the first to coin the term mindset, and his words ring true even today.

"I know we can do it" was part of my mindset; that positivity pushed me forward and won the respect and trust of people around me.
To this day, when faced with a difficult problem, even when options seem limited, I still say:

"I know we can do it."

Mindset shapes how we see the world. For example, a novelist's mindset is focused on finding and telling stories. Everywhere they look, they see narratives. Meanwhile, a chemist sees reactions, an account manager sees networks, and a therapist sees patterns of behavior.

As security professionals, our minds are set on finding threats. We spot risks, flaws, and vulnerabilities others miss. That's our strength—but it can also be our weakness.

Many security experts I've worked with have a "this is flawed" mindset. It's essential for identifying problems, but constant negativity can alienate colleagues. People tune out when all they hear is what's wrong.

The most effective security experts balance problem-finding with solution-building. They combine skepticism with optimism. They can say, "Here's the risk" *and* "Here's how we fix it."

But why would that matter? Shouldn't a cybersecurity professional's worth be measured by their code, not their mindset?

Not anymore.

Research done by Antwerp Management School showed that the most significant factor in effective business information security is not the sophistication level of protection against viruses or hackers; it's how committed senior management is to cybersecurity. When company culture and leadership sets the right tone, success follows. Technical solutions are great, but foundational support from stakeholders is the true driver of change.

In cybersecurity, this matters more than in almost any other IT field—because our work is complex, rarely the organization's top priority, and often requires relentless persuasion to get things moving. When protecting our organizations, we must convince others to make the right decisions. Gone are the days when a lone security genius could hole up and build the perfect antivirus. Today's professionals need to win support, rally teams, and inspire secure behavior across an organization.

Think about Gandalf in *The Lord of the Rings*. His greatest challenge wasn't fighting enemies—it was convincing leaders to prepare for the coming war. Many distrusted him because he always brought bad news. But he didn't need to win every kingdom; he just needed to "move the needle" enough to gather an army. Cybersecurity works the same way. We won't convince everyone of every risk, but if we can inspire enough action, we can build the momentum needed for real change.

A strong, forward-looking mindset isn't optional; it's the key to making progress.

This book proposes a transformative approach: integrating information security skills with strategic business alignment, proactive risk management, and continuous adaptation. The modern cybersecurity knight must don the mantle of a diplomat and a strategist, able to translate the esoteric scribbles of risk assessments and threat reports into stirring speeches that rouse stakeholders from their complacency.

The 11 characteristics in the chapters ahead aren't about learning new technical tricks. They're about building the mindset to evolve from guardians of IT to leaders in business strategy, viewing challenges as opportunities for growth and innovation. Effective leadership in cybersecurity is not just about managing technical teams but also about influencing company-wide strategies and fostering an environment that prioritizes cybersecurity practices.

Developing the diverse skillset highlighted throughout this book will prepare you to become one of the next generation of cybersecurity leaders. With the right mindset, we can shift from merely identifying threats to leading the charge in protecting what matters most.

THE 10 CHARACTERISTICS

Traditionally, cybersecurity has been perceived as a battle of firewalls and antivirus software, a technical trench war against malicious attacks. This paradigm dictated that the more technically skilled a security expert was, the more value they could provide.

That world has changed.

Sophisticated artificial intelligence and automation technologies have taken over routine tasks that used to occupy security teams. Malware detection, spam filtering, and anomaly flagging are done faster and more accurately by machines than by humans. As tools improve, the value curve for purely technical skills has flattened. Beyond a certain point, more technical depth no longer equals more impact.

The graph below shows how different the playing field is today from 25 years ago. In 2000, you generated more value the higher your technical skill was; today, the value flattens out no matter how high your skill.

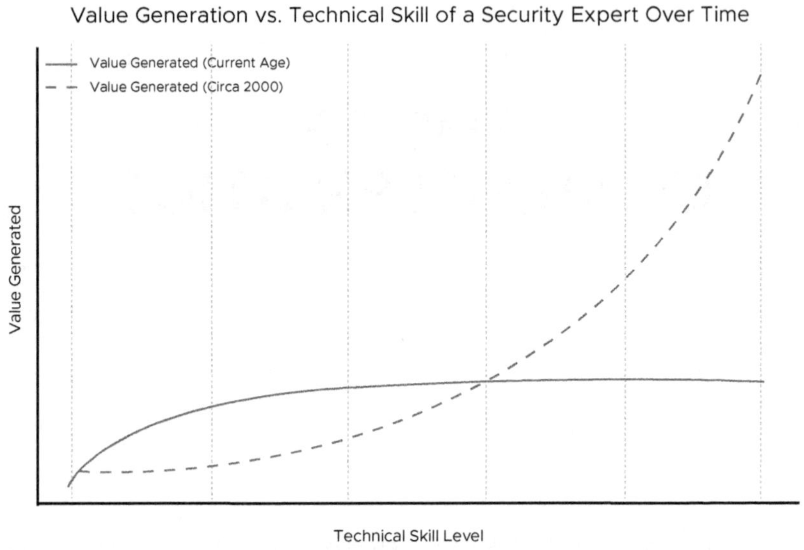

Figure 1 Fictive graph to showcase the diminishing returns of technical skills in our current age vs around 2000.

This is because our security tools are improving, and security experts are expected to deal with *new* risks as opposed to more *advanced* risks. Today, we trust the software that we spend our valuable cash on to deal with malware and spam, and turn our attention to topics like risk management, improving employee behavior, supply chain management, and so much more.

At the same time, organizations themselves have become more complex. A single decision about security can ripple through dozens of departments, supply chains, and partners. It's no longer just about keeping systems running; it's about ensuring business resilience, customer trust, and regulatory confidence all at once. In this environment, our value doesn't come only from what we know technically—it comes from our ability to influence, adapt, and lead.

This shouldn't come as a surprise; a proxy trend we can look at is the regulations published over the years. Back in the day, we might get one regulation every decade. Now, we see multiple new regulations almost every year. And these regulations don't demand a better firewall or a better anti-virus. They require communication, plans, and processes — all business topics. Of course, as the tools grow more sophisticated, so do the tools used by hackers and other bad actors. The rules of this game are being rewritten constantly; and as new cybersecurity tools flood the market, we in the industry simply cannot test out each and every one to verify if it's the real deal. This overwhelm can lead to insecurity on our part and distrust on our clients' part.

And while their distrust may not be earned, they have good reason to be anxious about their information security. Shareholders and business owners are asking for cyber protection to keep their money from disappearing into some hacker's pockets, bringing profits to a halt. Smaller businesses especially lack the financial backbone to withstand a cyber attack — that is one horrible way to lose the family business.

Which makes it all the more frustrating when the biggest impediment to a robust information security protocol is a client's inaction.

I learned this firsthand as a data scientist for a cybersecurity firm. My AI models were great; they could detect abnormal user behavior with unnerving precision. But I soon found that they couldn't save my clients from themselves. When I reported my findings, no one did anything. And it wasn't just my detections; this happened to all alerts, even simple ones like "Malware detected". They didn't understand the risk, and they didn't know what to do with the information I gave them. Even the clients who knew how to organize against security threats wouldn't prioritize it over their other work.

It wasn't because they didn't care; it was because they didn't see the business impact of failing to act.

But if the solution isn't a new tool or technique, what is it?

I've seen the tendency among my colleagues—brilliant cybersecurity professionals—to more or less give up. They throw up their hands, disheartened. But I believe that this new environment gives us the opportunity to redefine and reframe our role.

Instead of blaming our stakeholders for not understanding, we need to take back control. We must learn to compensate for our organizations' limitations, filling the gaps before they even appear.

And that requires a mindset shift.

The most effective security experts today bridge the gap between technical capability and organizational action. They don't wait for stakeholders to change their mindset; they work within the reality of the business to create change now.

The graph below shows the impact of these changes on the value we can generate via non-technical skills. Business savvy and communication skills are rapidly becoming the main source of value generated by information security professionals. Only in large tech companies does deep technical specialization still provide exceptional value, but even there, business skills are rising in importance.

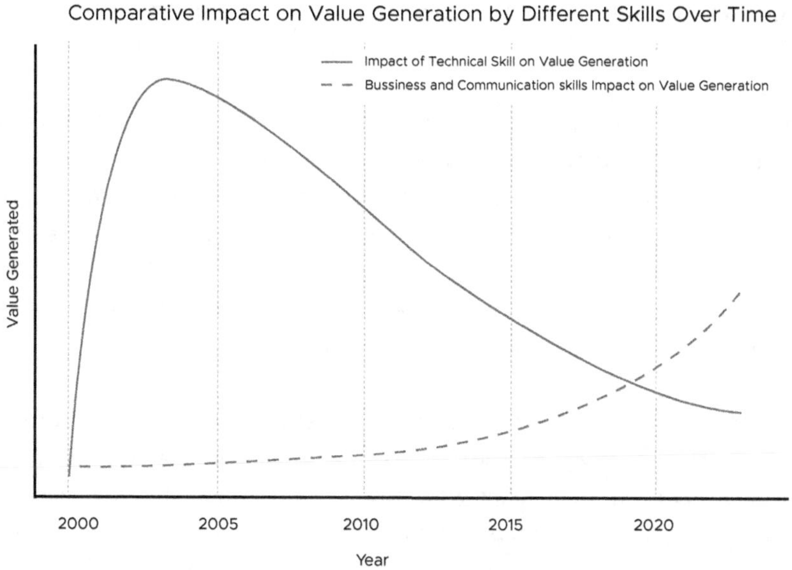

Figure 2 Fictive graph shows the impact of our skills on the value we generate as security experts.

THE MODERN SECURITY EXPERT

There is a clear pattern among those who consistently made an impact in their organizations. They shared a set of traits—not just skills, but ways of thinking and behaving—that allowed them to thrive in this new environment.

They are strategic in their approach, collaborative in how they work with others, and people-oriented in everything they do.

Their success doesn't come from knowing every detail of every system but from how they behave when uncertainty strikes, how they make decisions with imperfect information, and how they influence others to act.

They carry themself with quiet confidence and are not afraid to make decisions—even bold ones—when it matters most. They see the bigger picture, understanding what truly creates value for an organization and how to deliver it.

They know how to communicate so others can actually hear them. They read a room as easily as they read a log file, adjusting their approach so they can bring people with them instead of fighting alone. They manage their work in a way that gives others a sense of clarity and control, showing results instead of excuses. They translate the arcane language of IT security into tactical insights that resonate with stakeholders, turning complex problems into understandable and actionable information.

They focus on what matters most, choosing carefully where to spend their time and energy. They think ahead rather than ruminating, refusing to spiral into negativity even when things go wrong. In conversation, they stay flexible and curious, finding paths forward rather than trying to win every argument.

Their vision aligns with the organization they serve, and they never lose sight of the root of a problem, refusing to get stuck in details that don't matter. They stay organized, and they adapt—not just to new threats, but to new roles, new cultures, and new ways of working.

All of this leads to one conclusion: being an effective security expert today is no longer about knowing every command or mastering every framework. It's about who you are and how you operate.

The 10 characteristics we'll explore in this book encompass all of the above, and then some. Each trait captures a way of thinking and behaving that separates the most effective security experts from the rest. This isn't a checklist you can memorize; it's a way of seeing your role—a shift from "I fix problems" to "I shape outcomes."

10 NEXT-GEN CHARACTERISTICS

1. Valuable: Understands, identifies, and delivers meaningful value.
2. Efficient: Maximizes value relative to effort.
3. Perceptive: Reads the room and pivots when necessary.
4. Persuasive: Persuades others without imposing his will.
5. Optimistic: Thinks forward and avoids cycles of negativity.
6. Analytical: Reasons back to root causes without getting lost in irrelevant details.
7. Methodical: Maintains strong organization and structured thinking.
8. Reliable: Manages projects effectively, maintains control, and delivers results.
9. Bold: Dares to make decisions and act with conviction.
10. Adaptable: Adjusts easily to new roles and organizational cultures.

CHANGING YOUR MINDSET

You can't download a new mindset like an app; you can watch every motivational video on YouTube, sign up for every online course, read this very book ten times, and still find yourself stuck in the exact same place six months later. You will learn *about* a mindset from this book, but you can't learn a mindset. You have to teach it to yourself.

I've met brilliant people with good intentions who binge-watch productivity videos late at night, their browser full of tabs promising "5 hacks to level up your life" or "7 secrets to confidence." They nod along, feel inspired for a moment, maybe even buy a notebook to start fresh on Monday. But by Wednesday, they're back where they started—too busy, too distracted, too... unchanged.

The problem isn't that the videos are bad or the advice is wrong. The problem is simple: a mindset is lived, not learned. You don't "get" confidence by watching someone else be confident. You don't "become bold" because someone gave you a list of bold things to say. Those things are external; mindset lives inside. And the only person who can install it is you.

One thing productivity-junkies will tell you; mindset often boils down to nothing more than a sentence that gives you a specific way of looking at the world. You take this sentence into each scenario you face, applying it no matter the challenge, until it's so ingrained in your psyche that it becomes a part of your natural, instinctual behavior. At first, you consciously choose to look at the world through the lens of the sentence; over time, it becomes unconscious and reflexive.

Like a (security system?) that runs in the background, humming as it secretly protects the entire system, your mindset can protect you from stressors, from fears that hold you back, from external changes and self-sabotage. Of course, a negative mindset can make all those things worse.

Somewhere in your head, you might already have these sentences running:
"I need to avoid mistakes,"

"I'm not a people person,"

"If I don't know everything, I'll fail."

These sentences are like invisible filters. They decide what you notice, how you feel, and what you do. You probably didn't choose them on purpose. They came from experiences, people, maybe even fear.

The power of deliberately improving a mindset is choosing a sentence on purpose. Replacing "I need to avoid mistakes" with "I take bold action, even if it means failing sometimes." Or swapping "I'm not a people person" with "I connect easily with others."

Make no mistake; even if it can be boiled down to "a sentence", changing your mindset is still a system overhaul. You can't reprogram your entire brain overnight. People try—usually in January. They make huge lists: wake up at 5 a.m., run every day, eat better, learn a new language, become confident, read a book a week, meditate, journal... By February, the list is gone, and they feel worse than when they started.

You can't and shouldn't try to adopt all of the 11 characteristics at the same time. You need to be able to give the bulk of your attention to one concept, one mindset shift, at a time in order to truly allow it to change your behavior. Think of it like tuning a guitar. You don't grab all six strings at once—you tune one, and the whole instrument sounds better. Your mind works the same way.

Stop trying to overhaul your entire identity in one weekend. Pick one thing to change. Focus on it. Live it until it becomes automatic. Then move to the next one. That's how lasting change happens—one trait, one sentence, one deliberate shift at a time.

Though, that begs the question: "Which characteristics should I focus on?" Like it or not, there's an easy answer to that question: the one you're most dreading.

The characteristics that you fear most bring the most treasure. This is one of the core ideas of my other book, *Dragon Fire Method*, where I talk about how you will always find the treasures you seek buried within the subject you fear the most — your dragon.

A dragon is a representation of human fears combined into one made-up beast; in stories, dragons sit on huge hordes of gold and gemstones.

It's never the beautiful, benevolent unicorn that stands between you and your prize; it's the dragon, those fears and mental blocks that we feel insecure about.

For years, I avoided working on my social skills. I told myself it didn't matter: "I'm a technical person, I don't need to be great at networking." It sounded logical, but it wasn't. It was fear. The truth was, I felt awkward in social settings, and instead of facing it, I built a wall of excuses to avoid it.

Then one day, I realized that wall was costing me. Opportunities were passing me by, and I was the one holding the door shut. That's when I chose to face it. It was uncomfortable. It felt unnatural. But over time, those conversations that once terrified me became normal.

That one shift didn't just improve my social skills; it improved everything. I became more confident, better at influencing people, and even better at solving problems because I finally understood the people behind them.

So, choose the characteristic that breathes fire at you and dedicate yourself to improving that first. Come up with one sentence that represents the mindset you want to adopt. Keep it short enough to remember and strong enough to guide your choices. Maybe it's: "I make bold decisions," "I connect easily with others," or "I reason back to the root of the problem."

Write it down. Say it to yourself every morning. Put it on a sticky note where you'll see it every day. Then take one small action aligned with it before the day ends. That's it. No big declarations, no dramatic changes overnight—just one sentence and one deliberate choice.

Mindset change happens in the small moments. If your chosen sentence is "*I make bold decisions,*" start with something as simple as crossing one unimportant task off your list and refusing to do it. If your sentence is "*I connect easily with others,*" start one short conversation a day. Tiny steps feel small, but they stack up fast.

When the mindset starts to feel like second nature, push it further. That same boldness you practiced on your calendar? Use it in meetings. That conversation habit? Turn it into building stronger relationships at work. The first small steps create a foundation so you can take bigger ones without feeling like you're faking it.

Changing your mindset isn't instant, but it is reliable. One sentence, one habit, one situation at a time—until it's not something you think about, it's just something you do.

And remember; mindsets aren't tattoos. They're tools. You don't adopt one sentence and carve it into stone forever—you pick one up, use it, and when it's part of you, you move to the next.

You're allowed to adjust as needed. Maybe you choose *"I am brave and make bold decisions"* but realize after a few weeks that what you really need is *"I communicate clearly and read the room."* That's not failure. That's learning.

Flexibility keeps you from becoming rigid. A fixed mindset—even if it's positive—can still trap you. If you lock yourself into *"I am the brave one who always takes charge,"* you might bulldoze people when listening would have been better. By being willing to revisit and refine your mindset sentences, you stay adaptable—just like the cybersecurity environment we work in.

The point is progress, not perfection. Pick a mindset. Practice it in small, daily actions. Notice where it helps and where it doesn't. Adjust, refine, and when it's natural, move on to the next one.

It will feel small at first; almost too small to matter. But days stack into weeks, weeks into months, and soon you'll notice you've changed—not because you read about a mindset, but because you lived it.

So, choose your sentence now. Write it down. And tomorrow morning, act on it. Your dragon is waiting, and behind it is the treasure you've been looking for all along.

VALUABLE

Understands, identifies, and delivers meaningful value.

What is the value of information security?

If you ask the web, you get some pretty lame answers. The first article you will find says something like, "Protecting the integrity of information is critical." Information security is often simply something you must do and not doing it is "stupid!"

This might be true, but it doesn't help us understand the value of information security. Like anything else, information security has value.

For our purposes, let's define "value" as the measurable or perceived benefit an organization or individual gains from an action or investment. It can be tangible, like increased profit, or intangible, like reduced risk or improved reputation.

In cyber, the value we create is not always clear. "Creating digital safety" isn't as obvious as "selling 100,000 units this month."
That is why it is so hard to convince people to invest in cybersecurity. They can't see the relationship between the investments they're making and the

supposed increase in safety or reduction in risk. With sales, it's extremely easy. You're either making money or not, and there are ways to calculate and hypothesize the value easily.

Still, many companies *do* invest in information security when they could have used the money for something else, like marketing or starting an innovative project that is guaranteed to drive profit. So, there must be *some* utility. But what? Can it be quantified?

Investors are continuously trying to value businesses; looking at their methods might give us a hint. The underlying principle of investing is a simple calculation:

Expected return of an investment = risk X reward.

Investors expect a return against the risk they are taking. Their job is to minimize risk and maximize reward.

Well, information security doesn't increase the reward for investors (unless you're an information security provider). But it *can* impact the risk that an investor faces. Risk profiles are diverse and complicated—there's market, financial, geopolitical, operational and regulatory risks, just to name a few. Information security can play a role in several of those factors. Cybersecurity can reduce operational risks by keeping hackers out of logistical and inventory systems. It can minimize regulatory risk by showcasing robust consumer data protection to regulators. Combating spyware can keep competitors from collecting information on proprietary research or new products set to launch. It can even mitigate some financial risks, such as losing liquidity because a hacker group demands a big sum of money.

Risk reduction, then, has inherent value, and can contribute to the value of information security.

And this kind of thinking works.

The CEO of a security firm I once worked at was immensely good at selling the value of cybersecurity as risk-reduction. He would walk into soon-to-be clients' offices with the same pitch: "We take a risk-based approach to cybersecurity that drives value better than the old-fashioned way of 'just do it'." They all took the bait. Why? Because they all had issues showing value to their bosses. Top management wants to see how information security generates profit; understanding and prioritizing risk reduction is the only way to tell which investments are essential and which are a waste of money.

Any information security professional can rattle off reasons why their work is important; the trick is translating those reasons into something that makes sense to stakeholders. When you focus on the value of risk-reduction, you're speaking a language that executives can understand.

I learned this early in my career as a consultant. I'd been working at REVEN—a clothing brand—for six months. The IT manager, Daniel, and I had spent that time finding gaps in their cybersecurity posture and improving small flaws that didn't require additional investment.

We had some amazing wins during the process: we managed to find and resolve gaps related to suppliers, found that some applications had backups enabled, and figured out what the most critical assets were and how they tied to the business.

I was proud of my first real consultancy project; a project I managed to sell based on my own agile security approach and a process that I knew would work, even with a busy IT manager who only had a one or two hours to spend on it each week.

I completely understood the framework we were using and the CIS Controls, and my assessment of the gaps was the result of diving deep, asking questions, and performing technical analyses. In short, I had worked my ass off for this client.

Now, we were scheduled to present our findings to the CFO; he wanted to know what we'd been up to, and we needed funding to fix some of those gaps we'd found.

For me, this was great. It was my first time presenting to a C-level. I had just started doing consulting, and I finally had the chance to prove I had the skills to do the job.

I made sure to have the deck polished like glass; six months of work distilled into ten crisp slides—color-coded, risk-scored, CIS-mapped. Everything a security-conscious exec should want. I even shaved the jargon, swapped acronyms for clarity. My gut told me we nailed it.

Then, a week before meeting with the CFO, Daniel and I had a digital meeting with the new CTO, Hans, to go over the presentation. He'd worked for other large retail companies before and, just like me, he was ready to use this project to show his worth. That turned out to be an issue.

The meeting kicked off with Daniel and I trading our usual banter about the weather—it's tradition. It happened to be a bright, sunny day. REVEN's office building was gorgeous: huge windows, killer view when the sky's clear.

Hans logged in. Camera on. Posture straight. He nodded once.

I kicked things off with slide one: Context, approach, goals.

Then Daniel took over. He walked through the quick wins—our supplier cleanup, the backup fixes, the critical asset mapping. He sounded relaxed, confident. We were a team, and it showed.

Slide five rolled up—what we've already completed vs. what still needed investment. I laid it out clean: no fluff, just facts.

That's when Hans interrupted.

"Where are the stories?" His tone was sharp. "This is all technical nonsense." Stories? I wasn't a writer; I was an information security consultant. What did I know about stories?

"We haven't prepared any stories," I replied.

"And why is a penetration test not part of the investments?" Hans continued.

At least I had an answer to that question: "The assessment doesn't show that that would be the right move for our budget. We know most of the crucial issues already, and we prefer to use that money on things we know we have to solve than a penetration test."

"No," Hans said, shaking his head. "We need one anyway, I have to show a report on the current state of cybersecurity."

Now, I was getting nervous. We had done the assessment, we had the data, we had the current state of cybersecurity—but this CTO wasn't satisfied.

Then Hans made a weird statement, and things started to click for me: "I know what needs to happen. I made a mistake trusting the big consultant firms before; their advice didn't work out. I'm not going to make that mistake again."

Now, I was getting even more nervous. He wasn't going to listen. He wanted to prove a point, maybe add the term "cybersecurity" to his CV for his next job.

"Sure," Daniel sighed, giving in. "We'll change the slides, we'll add the stories, and we'll see if we can add the penetration test. Vincent, can you make a draft?"

I understood where Daniel was coming from; he didn't want to risk his relationship with his new boss. But I felt horrible. Before, I was proud of our results and confident in our presentation. Now, I had one week to overhaul the entire deck and add a recommendation that we didn't believe in. I felt undermined by a CTO who didn't appreciate my skill and knowledge. Hans clearly wanted to prove that he was better than the "big consultants"—and me.

"How can I solve this?" I thought. The answer was simple: I'd solve it like I always did. I'd do what was asked of me, learn everything I could about it, and prove that I was up to the challenge.

I spent hours reading about storytelling, researching stories of similar retailers who'd been hacked. I put them all together and revamped them, over and over, until I was proud. When I sent the slides over to Hans and Daniel, Hans wanted even *more* storytelling. So I went back to the drawing board, revising and improving until the day before the meeting with the CFO.

All of my excitement and confidence leading up to the big meeting had been replaced by nerves. Hans' critiques had thrown me, and this was my first meeting with a C-level management. But I'd worked hard, and Daniel and Hans both approved of my final presentation, so I went into the meeting with my head and my hopes high.

I came out of it in the exact opposite condition.

The meeting had been a disaster. The CFO wasn't interested in what we had to say. He didn't even seem to pay attention, slumped in his chair with his eyes on the trees outside. When he was paying attention, it was only to interrupt me and ask: "how is this relevant to the company?"

The CFO's last words in that meeting were: "We need to rethink everything we've been doing so far."

Until the meeting with the CFO, I always managed to believe that if I increased my skills, people would value me more, I would get more respect, and I would find myself in higher positions. But in this situation, I realized, I couldn't have gained more knowledge or cybersecurity skills. No matter how much technical expertise I gained here, it wouldn't have worked.
Shortly after, the project that Daniel and I were both so proud of, was cancelled.

IDENTIFYING VALUE FOR INDIVIDUAL STAKEHOLDERS

Not everyone will be convinced by the same argument, because "value" is subjective. People attach different values to the same thing. For example, some people will gladly pay $2,000 for a new Macbook, but many people won't.

This gets more complicated when you're looking at a project with multiple stakeholders who all value different things. If you can't figure out what each person values, and how to convince them to value your work, you'll have a hard time making a case for your worth. At REVEN, Daniel and I valued the quality of our work, Hans valued his ego, and the CFO valued cost reduction above everything else.

So, while risk reduction is a great way to see the value of information security, it isn't the only one. Competitive and ambitious people might see cybersecurity as one of the more advanced things they can do to stand out.
Some people might see it as a way to impress their bosses, taking a proactive approach to protecting the organization.

Some will see it as only as valuable as the amount of headaches it can fend off; especially when it comes to getting regulators off their backs.

If you're lucky, you might work with someone who sees the intrinsic value of good-quality cybersecurity—but probably only if you're dealing with another IT professional.

And many, many clients just want peace of mind; laypeople often don't know exactly what they're up against when dealing with information security, and being able to allay their concerns is a great source of value.

ALIGNING VALUE WITH ORGANIZATIONS

As much as you want to be able to tailor your demonstration of cybersecurity's value to the individuals you rely on for funding or greenlighting certain project, it's equally as important to align your values with the organization as a whole.

I didn't fully understand this myself until I came across a study by Matias Bronnenmayer, Bernd W. Wirtz, and Vincent Götte: *Success Factors of Management Consulting*. The paper asked a simple question: "What really makes a consulting project succeed?"

Early in my own career, the consensus in the consulting industry was that the answer was obvious: trust. Build trust with the client, and you can overcome disagreements, manage expectations, and deliver success.

BUT THE DATA TOLD A DIFFERENT STORY.

From a survey of 255 companies and a statistical model that linked consultant behavior to client satisfaction, they found trust was not the top success factor at all. In fact, trust didn't even make the top three.

Instead, two factors stood out:

1. **Ability to perform** – the consultant's expertise and ability to deliver tangible outcomes quickly.
2. **Common vision** – alignment between the consultant's goals and the client's vision for success.

In their words, projects were most successful when consultant and client shared "a common understanding of objectives and deliverables," and when the consultant could actually execute on that vision.

In cybersecurity, this is where so many professionals trip up. We build strategies based on what we think is important: patch management, zero trust, advanced detection tooling, compliance frameworks. We're not wrong; these things do matter. But no one else at the organization wakes up thinking, "How do we perfect our patching strategy this quarter?"

The organization wakes up thinking:

- "How do we hit our revenue target?"
- "How do we cut costs without slowing growth?"
- "How do we protect our reputation and keep customer trust?"

If your cybersecurity program doesn't tie directly into one of those core drivers, it'll just become noise, a low-priority nuisance.

Alignment means taking whatever vision the business already has and wrapping cybersecurity around it like armor. If their focus is rapid innovation, your security vision must support safe, fast deployments. If their focus is cost control, your security vision must highlight efficiency gains and cost-avoidance benefits. If their focus is compliance because they're entering a regulated market, your security vision must accelerate that compliance without becoming an anchor.

If you skip this step, you're setting yourself up for constant friction: endless debates, underfunded projects, and the feeling that no one "gets" what you're trying to do.

Even if you figure out exactly what drives a client and tailor your pitch to their concept of value, it can still be hard to convince them that your work is a worthwhile investment. So much of cybersecurity happens invisibly, defensive moves against unknown enemies. How do you measure the unknown, and how do you get your client to see the value in something they don't really understand?

MAKING VALUE VISIBLE

There's a disconnect between what we're told our value should be and how it's actually perceived. Despite the industry's emphasis on keeping out hackers and improving system reliability, clients rarely see the value of what didn't happen—the viruses that didn't bring down the network, the spyware that didn't make their servers vulnerable, the malware that didn't compromise client information.

They measure results in visible outputs: a passed audit, a new firewall, a completed training program. They can see it, so they can assign it value.

Security is often seen as baseline expectations—essential but not exceptional. Like expecting electricity when you flip a switch, organizations assume their digital infrastructures are secure and operational by default. They don't fully appreciate the complexities involved in maintaining that standard.

Unless you can communicate it.

I once had a CISO client with technical expertise. He had the know-how, but his diverse job responsibilities meant he didn't have the time to judge the quality of work conducted by a previous freelancer.

He just knew that the detection tooling wasn't working as intended.

I fixed the issue within the first few hours—as it turned out, some of the logs weren't being parsed correctly. It started working again, and my job was done.

Or, it would have been if I didn't see other ways I could deliver value.

While looking at the system, I noticed that it wasn't built to serve the customer's needs. It was horribly complex, and the issue I had just solved would almost certainly reoccur, soon. Plus, the system's capabilities weren't being fully utilized.

Instead of walking away (and waiting for the call to come back and fix it, again), I offered my client three solutions:

1. Fix the current issues—low cost, but likely to break again.
2. Address structural flaws—medium cost, significantly reduced risk.
3. Redesign the system for full optimization—high cost, eliminated flaws, doubled coverage.

He chose option 3. Why? Because I quantified the benefits and allowed comparison. Too often, security pros default to the "best" solution without explaining alternatives—leaving stakeholders unable to measure value. They wind up unsure if they're being taken for a ride, sowing distrust and dissatisfaction even before the job begins.

You can also make your value more visible when you explicitly align it with strategic objectives. When you shift focus from merely preventing attacks to enabling business growth, you begin to see a different kind of value.

Years after my disappointing meeting at REVEN, I had the opportunity to work with another retail company, Forthrite. This time, I knew to expect that the CFO would see security as a necessary expense rather than a profit-driver. Understandably, it made him hesitant to put anything more than the bare minimum into the IT budget. But I knew the CFO would understand the growing importance of digital sales; more business was being conducted through digital channels than physical stores.

So, we conducted a thorough risk assessment and identified areas where security improvements would have the most significant business impact on digital sales. These were not the standard improvements, like a better detection system on employee laptops or standard phishing training—instead, we focused on factors like printers, warehouse Wi-Fi, payment systems and the mobile app.

We only found these vulnerabilities because we learned to understand their business on business terms, not technical security best practices. And, by doing so, we not only reduced threats but improved operational efficiency — making the mobile app more reliable, which boosted productivity and customer satisfaction.

When security is tied to strategy, it shifts from "necessary expense" to "business enabler." That's when stakeholders truly see its worth. Instead of saying, "We need to improve endpoint detection to reduce risk exposure," you say, "This will prevent system outages that cost us $250k an hour during peak business days." When we learn to communicate how cybersecurity can contribute to revenue growth, customer satisfaction, and brand reputation, we can shift the conversation from expense to investment.

To help you apply this approach, the Appendix includes detailed tools that break down risk assessment and shows how to align security improvements with client value, along with a closer look at what worked at Forthrite.

Knowing the value of cybersecurity doesn't just help you show clients what they're getting and why it matters; it also helps *you* understand your role in a greater network. Carry this with you: your job isn't only about firewalls and frameworks, it's about translating invisible defenses into visible business value. That means listening harder than you talk, aligning your work with what actually drives the business, and tailoring your pitch to what each stakeholder cares about. When you frame security as an enabler of growth, efficiency, or peace of mind—whatever the audience values—you stop being the person who "costs money" and start being the person who helps the business grow (or, at least, protects its growth). That's the shift that will define how far you go.

DAILY MICROPRACTICE

I know my worth and the worth of cybersecurity, and I can demonstrate that worth to others

1. Translate Tech Into Business

   Before every presentation or email, take one technical point you want to make and rewrite it in business terms. Example: change "improve endpoint detection" into "avoid $250k/hour losses from downtime." Do this until it's second nature.

2. Stakeholder Mapping

   Make a quick grid of your stakeholders. One column for names, one for what they value most (cost reduction, reputation, innovation, ego, etc.). Before pitching, tailor your framing to hit their personal definition of "value."

3. Visible Wins

   Always deliver something visible in the short term—a passed audit, simplified report, or resolved vulnerability—while you work on the deeper, invisible security improvements. People trust what they can see; give them proof early.

EFFICIENT

Maximizes value relative to effort.

Your time is limited, as is your team's and your stakeholders' time. To be the best information security professional you can be, you need to be resourceful and efficient, maximizing value versus effort. That sounds simple, but too often we lack the mindset to do it.

I once worked with a security engineer named Marco. He was technically brilliant, but had deadline-blindness.

"A good Security Operation Center needs, of course, to know every asset and risk," he said as we started planning our project. "The entire system needs to be connected. Otherwise, we'll miss attackers."

"Eh, sure," I said, doing the mental math on what it would take to pull off Marco's plan. In theory, he was right. In practice, we had one month. "But our asset database isn't up-to-date. Do you want to start with that?"

"Yes," he said. "And then we need to know the risks of each asset and their impact on the business. Ingest all this data in the SIEM."

"Which do you want to prioritize?" I asked. "We can update asset management, or we can add critical log sources. Which one matters most?"

"All of it," he said. "It doesn't have to be perfect, but we need to start."

I've had identical conversations, more times than I can count.

As security experts, we have a tendency to get overwhelmed by all the work on our plates. "Protecting our systems and data" is a very clear goal with a very unclear path to success. We have no clue where bad actors will launch an attack, so we try to cover every inch, doing everything we can think of. This simply doesn't work.

Security is an endless buffet of problems. Assets, risks, logs, monitoring, detection—there's no finish line. In my experience, trying to do too many projects at once leads to your organization's defense losing ground with each battle — you will die by a thousand cuts, from yourself.

Let's pretend cybersecurity is a sport, with points given and deducted based on defense projects. Failing a project might lead to 10 points taken away, while a half-finished project that doesn't do much once its implemented nets you a measly 5 points. But, a strategic project that defends at the highest level? That's 1,000 points. You'd need 200 so-so projects and not a single failure to get to that score. If you aim to win, you should concentrate your attention on where you can make the most difference.

My project management teacher once said: "Take a task. Estimate the time. Then double that estimation. Take that number and double it again, and then you have a suitable estimation."

He might have been exaggerating a bit, but he wasn't far from the truth. Things always take more time than expected.

That's why efficiency isn't about doing everything—it's about doing the right things.

Trying to do assets, risks, and connecting them to the SIEM all at once won't work, and you'll spread the team so thin they won't be able to complete anything on time. When the deadline comes and you have nothing but half-finished work to present, stakeholders learn that they can't trust you to deliver. And, if they can't trust you, why would they give you more support or money for new projects?

Instead, we need to see which of our projects and tasks will provide the most value, and focus only on those. Each task should be checked against its value: how much time and effort will this take, relative to its contribution to the overall worth of the project?

And we need to develop a mindset of *exclusion* rather than *inclusion*. Be liberal in your decision not to do something that isn't absolutely necessary to the success of the project as a whole.

When a stakeholder asks for a specific task to be included, ask him why. If he gives a good answer, ask him again. Refuse if you can, and if you can't, take your trusted Gantt chart and show how including this task will impact your project. If possible, negotiate a trade, replacing the requested task for another that will be more valuable; protect your project as much as you protect the business against hackers. Ultimately, you're protecting stakeholders' interests, even if it means protecting them from themselves.

This method also keeps you sane during big, time-consuming projects. By maximizing your value, you keep your own planning in check, avoiding burnout or stress. This isn't just for your mental health; it's good business practice. Calm, focused professionals deliver more than stressed, chaotic ones.

This all starts by identifying hidden value. Value can be like a buried treasure, unknown to those who don't have the map to find it.

One of the easiest ways to find hidden value? Ask.

This is where most security professionals stumble. We assume everyone sees the world like we do: risk scores, vulnerability ratings and patch cycles. But stakeholders rarely think in those terms. They think in outcomes: revenue, costs, and reputation.

Instead of walking into meetings with your own plan already set in stone, walk in with questions like:

- "What's keeping you up at night?"
- "What does success look like for you this quarter?"
- "If you had to choose between speed, cost, or security right now, which one matter most?"

You'll be amazed at what people say when you actually ask. Some want control, some want compliance because regulatory fines keep them awake at night, and some want speed because their company is growing so fast they fear technology will bottleneck their expansion.

Once you know their vision, you can align cybersecurity to support it instead of competing with it.

For example, I was once hired to restore a SIEM system that hadn't been maintained for a long time. It was a hell of a job—cloud connectors, server logs, endpoint feeds, even an extra security module. It looked impressive but was unmanageable.

"You've got quite a large, complex system," I said to the client. "And a lot of these things are cool. But what do you really need? What are you trying to do with this system?"

He looked pleased, like no one had asked him that question before.

"Actually, I'm trying to monitor this specific application for our board members. And I need some control over admin accounts in the Windows system."

"So, you don't need all of this," I said, listing some of the installed features, like the extra security module.

"No" he replied. "When you say it like that, no, I really only need these specific features, and I'd prefer to keep them simple enough for me to tune and search when possible".

"Perfect," I replied. "Then I can save myself lots of time and you lots of money. We're going to uninstall and cleanup all the features you don't need and focus only on the things that matter."

The client gave me a huge smile, as if it was his first time receiving such a simple answer. He agreed.

Instead of focusing on adding more, I focused on doing less and cleaning up. My time was maximally valuable, and I focused only on those things that mattered the most.

Hidden value isn't only about cutting clutter. Sure, stripping out the noise saves time and sanity, but that's just one flavor. You can discover value in reusing tools you already have, or matching people with work within their strengths, or by simply motivating people to do the job.

And don't just weigh tasks in hours. Time isn't cheap, but neither is energy. A one-hour job that melts your top engineer's brain for the rest of the day costs way more than a three-hour grind your intern can script away happily. Some tasks build momentum, others drain it. If you only measure the clock, you'll miss the bigger toll—the afterburn that lingers when people are fried. Efficiency isn't just about speed, it's about sustaining energy so you can keep delivering past this sprint.

The same goes for showing value to clients. They don't feel "time saved" unless you make it visible. Translate every trade-off into their language: money they didn't have to spend, downtime they dodged, fines they avoided.

Contrast the messy "before" with the streamlined "after." Say, "Because we skipped that module, you got monitoring live two months earlier." That sticks. Stakeholders rarely thank you for invisible wins—you've got to hold up the mirror.

Maximizing value doesn't mean doing less for the sake of less. Find the spots where effort hits hardest, where energy is best spent, and double down there. Exclude, focus, deliver, and make sure the people paying the bill know precisely what they gained. When you do that, security stops looking like overhead and starts looking like leverage.

DAILY MICROPRACTICE

I know how to identify the hidden value in a project.

1. **The "Matter" Check**
   Before starting any task, ask: "Does this really matter?" If yes, green light. If no, reconsider.

2. **The Energy Audit**
   Don't just estimate hours—estimate energy burn.
   Tag tasks as light, medium, or heavy lift. Then stagger them: never pile two heavy lifts back-to-back on the same person. Treat energy like a budget, and always keep it in the black.

3. **The Stakeholder Echo**
   When you cut or reprioritize something from a project, translate it back to your clients' language immediately:
   - "This saves you $X in license costs."
   - "This gets your team live two weeks earlier."
   - "This avoids unnecessary risks."

That echo turns invisible security wins into visible business value.

PERCEPTIVE

Reads the room and pivots when necessary.

The room was already warm, and not just because of the bad AC. The CFO on the other side of the table was looking at my colleague, Thomas, with a blank stare, but he just continued his story. Meanwhile, the IT manager was frantically fidgeting with a pen.

"Doesn't he see it?" I wondered.

He didn't. Of course he didn't. He was knee-deep in technical sludge, wading through system failures and data inconsistencies like he was debugging with words. His voice pitched higher, thinner, the way voices do when desperation leaks in.

The CFO blinked slowly.

Thomas doubled down. Acronyms, logs, post-mortems. He was trying to prove he was right, but he didn't see that he'd already lost

"This isn't about system uptime," I said, jumping in. "It's about trust. From your side, if the system fails again during quarter close, it's not just a tech problem—it's a credibility problem. I get that. What we're proposing ensures you don't have to explain any more delays to our customers."

Her chin lifted, just a notch. But I saw it.

Now we were speaking her language.

She nodded once: *Go on.*

But the IT manager wasn't as readily calmed.

"Okay, okay," he cut in. "But we need to know if that server is vulnerable, right *now*."

Thomas froze, then went textbook. I bit back a groan.

"I can't say yet. We need more data before I can answer that."

The temperature in the room spiked. The manager leaned back, crossed arms, lips pressed tight.

You could feel the frustration creep up from his shoulders into the air like static.

"I have to report something today," the IT manager said. "Deadline's tomorrow. What can we recommend?"

Thomas straightened in his chair, voice firm. The CFO lifted an eyebrow, glancing between Thomas and the IT manager.

"No," Thomas said. "We have to research first. That's the only way to know for sure."
I knew that Thomas wasn't wrong. He was right about needing more data. But he wasn't able to see what the IT manager was asking for and deliver

something close enough to mollify him, and it was making us look useless.

“We don’t have full data yet,” I said, jumping in. “But here’s what we know. If the server is vulnerable, the biggest risk is unauthorized access that could expose sensitive data. Short-term, we can block external access to reduce exposure immediately. Long-term, we validate with full research to confirm and patch if needed.”

And just like that, trust was returned—the CFO knew enough to feel confident we were doing our job, the IT manager had something to present by his deadline, and Thomas and I hadn’t undercut our own principles or processes.

This was a turning point for me; it proved that reading the room was a superpower. I would continue to use this superpower throughout my career, influencing top CEO’s, CTO’s, and all other types that start with a capital C.

Many security experts have a background in IT or are still focused on IT security, so they’ve gotten used to working with computers; most of the time, when you tell a computer to do something, it does it. And when it doesn’t, you have the code there to review so you can find out exactly what went wrong.

People aren’t like that. To communicate effectively with people, you need to be able analyze their feedback in real time. You need to know when to speak and when to stay quiet, and you need to know how to talk to people in ways they understand. You need to be able to say the right thing the first time you speak, or the conversation can veer wildly off-track.

It sounds like a lot of work—because, for many people, it is—but it is absolutely necessary. People cooperate more when they understand you, and cybersecurity is all about cooperation.

This is very much unlike other departments. An IT department might function better with cooperation from other colleagues, but it can largely succeed on its own, needing support from a limited set of stakeholders. Same goes for the marketing department, they can do their thing independently even of the IT, HR, sales or whoever doesn't cooperate with them. This might cause friction and disrupt the office politics, but it doesn't put the entire company at risk.

But in cyber, one of the risk factors is people and the way they behave. Many different departments need to be functioning in tandem, everyone doing their best to uphold information security protocol, in order for the project as a whole to be successful.

For example, I was assigned to help a large university in the Netherlands pass a security audit. We needed to coordinate with the IT department, legal, HR, local building managers and other external bodies, across fifteen different topics. There were more than ten teams in IT alone!

If you need something from a stakeholder, the best way to get it is to make sure they don't hate you. People don't like being talked down to, and they don't like feeling stupid. Throwing a lot of complex technical jargon at someone is a sure way to lose their interest and, potentially, make them feel insecure in their own intelligence.

Avoiding this is a matter of really understanding what people do in their departments. Instead of trying to make them understand *your* job, put in the effort to understand *theirs*. When I need to get a lot of different people from a lot of different departments on board, I learn about their daily work, challenges and goals.

At the large university, when I had so many different stakeholders to convince, I started by diving into what each department was up to. I read their project updates, skimmed through internal reports, and noted their key objectives. This groundwork helped me see things from their perspective, learn their internal lingo and priorities, and adjust my approach accordingly.

For marketing, I highlighted how cybersecurity protects customer data, which is crucial for their personalized campaigns and brand trust. I shared stories of companies that suffered reputational damage due to data breaches, making the risks real and underscoring the value of strong security.

Operations clearly cared about efficiency and reliability, so I focused on how cybersecurity prevents system outages and disruptions that could halt the supply chain. By framing security as a way to keep things running smoothly, they understood its importance to their workflow.

When I spoke with finance, I knew they'd respond to numbers, so I presented cybersecurity as an investment that prevents costly incidents like fraud or regulatory fines. By outlining potential financial losses avoided through strong security, I connected it directly to their goal of effective budget management. For human resources, protecting employee data was a top concern. I discussed how cybersecurity safeguards sensitive information and how security can help prevent nasty internal incidents like colleagues learning each others' salaries, aligning with their focus on maintaining a positive work environment.

By tailoring my message to each department, I made cybersecurity relevant to their specific needs and goals. It wasn't about changing the facts, but presenting them in a way that resonated with each team. Understanding what drove them allowed me to bridge the gap between technical security measures and business objectives. It turned abstract concepts into concrete benefits that everyone can appreciate.

In the end, this approach fostered stronger collaboration across the university. Departments started seeing cybersecurity not as a hurdle but as a partner in achieving their goals. This experience reinforced that being adaptable and empathetic is key in the ever-changing business landscape. By stepping into others' shoes and speaking their language, we can make cybersecurity not just a necessity but a valued part of the organization.

You also need to spend time learning about the individual people you're communicating with—especially when you're entering a high-stakes meeting.

Before you even walk into the room, you should think about all the pushback you might receive. You know what each person cares about, so anticipate where their attention will be directed. Who will want to know if it can be done cheaper? Who will want to know if a different system will be easier? Know how you'll respond to these arguments, and be prepared to confidently defend your plan against them.

But, as we saw at REVEN, you can have the perfect argument mapped out and still face resistance. It's very likely that you'll need to be able to gather real-time data about how well a meeting is going, and change your approach based on how the C-levels are responding.

Pay attention to body language—it's not an exact science, but you can train yourself to not only notice, but also interpret and understand, the minute details of someone's posture or facial expressions. This is a crucial part of active listening—the art of not just hearing, but truly understanding what someone is saying. Too often, we already know what we want to say and are just waiting for our turn to say it. That makes it all too easy to ignore an important point or trample over a concern that would be easily dispelled. Active listening means putting your response on the back burner so you can fully engage with the conversation that is actually happening, rather than the one you're having in your head.

For practical resources and research-backed exercises to help you "read the room", see the Appendix. Over time, with a mindset shift and a few tools, you'll build the instinct to adjust on the fly—making your arguments land where they count.

CONVERSATIONAL FLEXIBILITY: LEARNING TO PIVOT

So, now you know how to take the temperature of a room—but then what? Thinking on your feet, being able to pivot mid-meeting, is just as important as being a mind-reader. My colleague, Thomas, didn't falter because he lacked expertise. His mistake was locking himself into a corner and staying there. Three mistakes sealed the deal.

Mistake 1: Rigid Thinking – "I need research first, no exceptions"

Thomas came into that meeting with one script in his head: *no data, no decision*. It sounds safe, even responsible, but in a live conversation? It was a dead end. The client wasn't asking for perfect certainty; they were asking for direction in a critical moment. They'd handed over control of this project to us, and now they were asking for proof that they'd made the right choice in doing so. Thomas treated the conversation like a multiple-choice test where every choice was "no." That's rigid thinking: when you see only one valid path forward and refuse to adapt. Security pros love process (for good reason), but clinging to that process like it's gospel kills momentum. A flexible expert thinks: *What value can I add right now, even with partial data?*

Mistake 2: Silence Instead of Options

Even when you don't know everything, you can still map the field. What's likely? What's risky? What's the worst-case scenario? A quick outline helps stakeholders feel like they know what's going on, even if final confirmation comes later. Thomas offered none of that. He gave zero options, zero risk framing, zero next steps—just a blank wall. In security conversations, people crave clarity and control. If you don't give them something to work with, they will fill that silence with frustration, doubt, and distrust.

Mistake 3: Forcing His Way Instead of Guiding

When challenged, Thomas didn't pivot; he dug in. "No, we have to do research first. That's the only way." That language kills collaboration. It signals: *My way or nothing*. And the second you take that tone, you lose influence. Good security communication isn't about forcing compliance; it's about guiding people to their own conclusion while staying true to the facts. You lay out the choices, clarify the trade-offs, and let them pick a path they can own. That's how you gain trust. Thomas didn't guide; he dictated. The result? A defensive client and a stalled conversation.

Thomas didn't need to sacrifice his principles or try to tell the future; he just needed to be more flexible.

When the manager said, "We need a recommendation now," Thomas could've taken a breath and leaned in. Not with "No, we can't", but with something like my own response. That's flexible thinking. I didn't make any wild promises; I gave a provisional direction—something the client could act on immediately—while clearly laying out the need for proper validation.

Instead of a brick wall ("We can't answer until research is done"), I was a guide. I acknowledged the unknown, shared what is known, and laid out options: one quick move to calm the risk, one structured plan to lock it down for good. This instantly did three things:

1. **Relieved pressure.** The manager now had something to keep stakeholders happy.
2. **Built trust.** The client heard, "We're on your side and thinking with you, not against you."
3. **Kept control.** We stuck to our principles while steering the conversation instead of shutting it down.

That's the sweet spot: quick-thinking without overpromising, flexible without losing integrity. Meetings stop being brick walls and start being bridges.

Quick thinking doesn't mean pulling answers out of thin air. It means having the nerve to say, "Here's what we can do right now," even when you don't have the full picture. You connect past experience, core principles, and common sense. Then you craft a response that calms the room and keeps momentum.

Because here's the thing—if you don't offer a path forward, someone else will. And odds are, that path will be worse.

You can—and should—be flexible and empathetic in other forms of communication, as well. A large portion of the work we do and value we provide, especially if we're in a consulting role, is leaving a lasting impression in the form of written policies meant to keep an organization safe for years to come. But, I've found that policies often fail—not because people don't care, but because the statements inside them are lacking. They're vague or confusing, or way too dense and technical. They're written in a way that makes people stop and think, "Okay... but what do you actually want me to do?"

A client once proudly showed me their "Data Security Policy." It was one page long. One page. The entire company's approach to data security, from customer information to internal trade secrets, was defined in four bullet points. On paper, it looked "clean" and "easy to understand." In reality, it covered nothing meaningful.

On the other hand, I've also seen policies that read like legal novels. Fifty pages of definitions, sub-policies, nested exceptions, and flowcharts no one has time to read—let alone follow. They looked impressive, but ask an employee how to follow it and you'd get a blank stare. The policy was too broad and so complex that compliance was impossible.

A good policy considers the entire environment: technology, people, processes, and third parties. That means thinking beyond your own IT team and know how each department runs. How do suppliers access your systems? How do employees handle data on personal devices? How do your processes evolve as the business grows?

The people who implement your policies, from IT to accounting, all know the real workflow. They know what's possible, what's painful, and where the gaps really are. If you don't bring them into the conversation, you'll miss that reality.

Get their input before you finalize anything. Ask what challenges they face. Listen, even if their answers aren't what you expected. Maybe the rule you thought was simple actually needs new tools, or an extra person, or even a complete rethink of how work gets done. If your policy says "all critical systems must be patched within 24 hours" when half the applications in use need days of testing before a single update can safely go live, you're setting everyone up for failure.

Something else happens when you do this: people take ownership. They see the policy as their policy because they helped shape it. And that changes how they act. People are far more likely to follow a rule they helped create than one that just dropped into their inbox unannounced.

Many IT professionals gravitate to the field because they think it isn't a human-centric industry. For some roles, that's right. But for cybersecurity professionals, it couldn't be further from the truth. These days, communication is as vital to our job as writing code. The good news is that it's a versatile skill, and practicing it will help you in and out of the office. Social skills like being perceptive to others' subtle feedback, having the flexibility to respond and change tactics when your first plan falters, and speaking to people in their own language will take you farther than you think.

DAILY MICROPRACTICE

I read the room with ease and can think on my feet in response.

1. Practice Active Listening
   In one conversation each day, focus on listening more than talking. Watch body language, notice tone, and ask one question that shows you understand the other person's perspective. This builds awareness and teaches you to adapt your words to the situation rather than pushing your own agenda.

2. The Two-Sentence Rule
   When answering under pressure, cap yourself at two sentences max. First sentence: acknowledge concern. Second sentence: give direction. Anything longer risks spiraling into jargon or losing the

room. The second sentence can be vague, like "I don't know what the right solution is, but I know where to look."

3. The "If/Then" Buffer
   When pressed for certainty but you lack full data, default to a two-part line: "If X is true, then here's the quick step, but we might be flying blind. If not, here's the long fix." The long fix should then include gathering the data you don't know yet. That way you never freeze, and the room always gets direction.

PERSUASIVE

Communicates strategically to convince others

Chris had stayed late every night for a month, cleaning up a system no one else wanted to touch and fixing things most people didn't even understand. By the morning of his big meeting with the CFO, he was exhausted but confident. In the break room, he spoke with pride about the project. It was his baby, and he knew it inside out, describing everything in perfect, exacting detail.

I wished him luck in his meeting, not believing he'd really need it.
Turns out, he did.

When I saw Chris again that afternoon, he was heartbroken. The meeting had not gone the way he pictured at all.

"I don't know what happened," he said, shaking his head. "I gave her all the data, all the technical details. She was nodding and smiling the whole time, but at the end she just said 'I think we should switch technology, this is horrible'."

I wasn't in the meeting, but I had a good idea of what went wrong. Explaining in detail, showing the complexity he mastered, had only shown the CFO that the system was complicated, fault-prone, and bound to fail.

"And you couldn't convince her otherwise?" I asked.

Chris gave me an odd, annoyed look, like I was rubbing salt on his wounds.

"I didn't try," he said. "She's the CFO. I *know* I was right about everything, but she didn't see it that way. What else could I say to convince her?"

The truth is: plenty. But only if he knew how to persuade. Instead, once the CFO had expressed doubt in the system, Chris gave up. He wasn't comfortable trying to advocate for his project, or he didn't know how.

And he's not alone in that; persuasive speaking isn't normally a required part of the curriculum for a computer science degree. But, as I've learned over the course of my career, it probably should be.

Back when I was just starting out, before I turned to consulting, I spent most of my time programming. Programmers get taught one lesson more than any other: "the more knowledge you can translate into code, the harder you work, the more results you get." And it was true! Programming made me feel like a magician coming up with spells. I was changing the world with each keystroke; even if the world was just the screen in front of me. The faster I wrote my code, with more technical skills and more expertise, the more magic came out of my fingers.

When my career evolved, I took that same mindset with me into information security and consulting—knowledge was power, and being right would get me wherever I needed to go. I, like many security experts, fell back on "being right". I'd done the work and had the expertise; surely, that would translate to a successful conversation. After all, that's how computers work: the right code leads to the desired outcome.

I quickly found out that all those magical, world-changing spells only worked if I could convince others to believe in them. I needed to learn how to influence *people*; that, it turns out, is very different than learning to influence computers. Computers follow strict rules, lack personal motives, and are completely consistent—they are pure logic.

People are the exact opposite in every way. Often, people can't care less about your perfect technical answer, and insisting on your correctness can come off as patronizing or scolding—winning you more enemies than allies.

In the world of egos and motives, of boardrooms and alliances, effort doesn't equal impact. Think of meetings as mini-battles: if you enter the room with only your knowledge as armor, you won't fare well.

Once you've read the room and know where the conversation is heading, its time to use your pivoting skills to align the discussion in a way that favors you. But what if none of your approaches are working? That's where the 3T's Framework comes in—Teach, Tailor, Take Control.

THE 3T'S FRAMEWORK (TEACH, TAILOR, TAKE CONTROL)

This framework isn't mine. It comes straight out of the research behind *The Challenger Sale* by Matthew Dixon and Brent Adamson. They analyzed thousands of high-performing sales interactions and found one common thread: top performers don't just answer questions, they teach insight, tailor it to the person in front of them, and take control of the conversation without steamrolling anyone. That same approach works perfectly in cybersecurity conversations.

Teach.

Your job isn't to flex how much you know. It's to make someone else *get it.* No jargon or 20-minute lectures on buffer overflows. Keep it simple. Break security down into human language: risk, impact, action. "If this server is exposed, attackers can steal your data. Here's how that hurts your business."

That's it. If they understand it, they can act on it. If they don't, you just wasted oxygen. Teaching insight creates trust and drives action.

Tailor.

Put your flexibility and pivot skills to use. Remember, people come to the table with their own values: deadlines, budgets, egos. Adapt on the fly. If the CFO asks, frame the issue in dollars and liability. If the engineer asks, talk technical mitigations. If the manager says, "We need a decision today," show them what's safe enough for today. The research in *The Challenger Sale* showed that tailoring responses, matching the conversation to the other person's priorities, separates top performers from the pack.

Take Control.

Control isn't about bulldozing your point of view. It's about leading the conversation. Guide them through risk and options, and let *them* choose. Example: "Option A is quick and keeps you covered short term. Option B is deeper but takes time. Which fits your priorities?" You're steering, but you're not forcing. Ask questions that lead them to your conclusion—like the Socratic method—so they feel ownership of the decision. People rarely resist conclusions they've convinced themselves of.

And according to Dixon and Adamson, those who take control—not aggressively, but confidently—drive better outcomes and stronger relationships.

OTHER LENSES ON PERSUASION

The 3Ts are one way to think about persuasion. But they aren't the only way. If that framework doesn't click for you, there are other research-backed approaches worth keeping in your back pocket.

Aristotle's classic model of persuasion is simple but timeless: *ethos, pathos, logos*. Ethos is your credibility—why you are worth listening to. Pathos is your emotional connection—why they should care. Logos is your logic—why your idea makes sense. Most security professionals lean almost entirely on logos. They show charts, metrics, and technical details, then wonder why the argument falls flat. But if the person across the table doesn't trust you (*ethos*) or doesn't feel personally invested in the outcome (*pathos*), your logic won't land. Sometimes the fastest way to make a technical point stick is to slow down and establish credibility and empathy first. Remind them that they hired you for a reason, and that you want the same thing they do: for the organization to succeed.

Modern psychology backs this up. Robert Cialdini's research on influence found that people are moved by more than facts—they respond to cues like authority, consistency, and social proof. In practice, that might sound like: "Other companies in your sector are already adopting this control," or "Last quarter you said customer trust was your top priority; this step protects exactly that." When you link your proposal to their existing commitments or to what peers are already doing, you make it far easier for them to say yes.

And then there's storytelling. Studies show people retain stories up to 22 times more than raw facts. If you want a CFO to understand the risk, don't just cite a probability chart. Tell the story of the company who ignored the same warning and lost millions—or the story of how your team prevented a breach that could have been catastrophic. Stories humanize risk and turn abstract numbers into lived stakes.

If you're unsure which persuasion style fits you, here's a simple test: the next time you have to make a case, try boiling it down into a "60-Second Story." One sentence on the risk. One sentence on the impact. One sentence on what happened to someone else who ignored it. If you can deliver that without jargon, you've already gone further than most experts ever do.

Diplomacy in cybersecurity isn't about winning arguments. It's about leading conversations in a way that creates clarity, aligns with priorities, and moves people to act.

Chris had the expertise, but he didn't have the diplomacy. If he had taught simply, tailored his message, and taken control of the conversation, the CFO may have left that room convinced—not confused.

DAILY MICROPRACTICE

I am a persuasive communicator who teaches clearly, adapts flexibly, and leads conversations with confidence.

1. **Teach in Plain Language**
   Pick one technical concept from your day and explain it in 2–3 sentences without jargon. Test it on someone outside your field (a friend, partner, or even yourself aloud). If they get it, you've practiced clarity.

2. **Tailor on the Spot**
   In your next conversation, notice the other person's priorities (time, cost, reputation, etc.). Restate your point once, framed in their terms. For example: shift "This patch reduces attack vectors" to "This patch avoids downtime that could cost $20k an hour."

3. **Tell Your Story**
   Each time you have a "win", write down the story of what happened—not just the facts, but the people involved and the things at stake. Next time you need to persuade someone to do the same thing, you'll have a story ready to share about the last time it worked.

OPTIMISTIC

Thinks forward and avoids cycles of negativity.

The Security Operations Center was a room with three lines of desks, each outfitted with two or three screens. On the wall, a giant projection tracked firewalls and high-risk incidents. In front of it, my colleagues Frank and Oksana vented about a client.

"The customer doesn't know anything," Oksana said. "They don't even understand their own infrastructure and their systems are outdated. They're high-risk, and we have to protect that mess." "Not only that, they don't want to cooperate with us." Frank shook his head. "Did you see how the CTO tried to mesh with our proposals, shooting it all down? I don't think they want security, they just want to check a box."

I kept my thoughts to myself, but I doubted their perspectives were the whole story.

I think you've just been shooting down everything the customer has been working on, I thought. Maybe the client is underfunded, understaffed, and overwhelmed. Maybe they need help, not judgment.

"I don't think he cares at all," Oksana sighed.

Wow, I thought. What an assumption! That is not the right mindset to have.

We cybersecurity professionals tend to be a rather negative bunch. There's an argument to be made that having a pessimistic mindset helps us find threats; we're cynical and suspicious and always looking for flaws—no wonder we're so good at finding them.

But, at the same time, this negative mindset holds us back. It's one of the reasons people from other departments don't like working with security professionals: "they always tell use we're doing everything wrong" and "they come with more work and no regard for our time" are common refrains. I once saw a manager hiding under his desk to avoid having to interact with the security leader!

The good news? You actually can do both. Be critical when analyzing systems, but positive when presenting to people. You can switch on your fault-finding negative mindset when you're running an assessment, and shift to a more positive outlook when it's time to report back to a client or colleague.

Think of it as having a "negativity on demand, use only when needed" mindset.

Studies show that practicing optimism broadens thinking, sparks collaboration, and makes teams more resilient. In other words: it creates the conditions where security advice actually lands.

In most cases, it isn't the security expert who works directly with sensitive data and customers, or who configures servers and systems. Other people in the company are responsible for those elements of cybersecurity; we need to convince them to play ball in order to get anything done. And, clearly, constant criticism doesn't work to win them over. We need to switch up our approach to one of relentless positivity—with the occasional, well-timed and apt critical observation—in order to move security forward.

I learned this lesson during a project in which I was tasked with getting an organization ready for an upcoming audit. A security expert, Eli, was already working the project, but he wasn't getting results. The meetings he scheduled went unattended, and the changes he suggested were ignored.

After working with Eli, I figured out what was going on. People didn't like working with him. They found him overly critical; all he ever talked about was what they were doing wrong, how they needed to improve, and harangued them to start making his prescribed changes.

The result? People tuned him out.

Eli's negative mindset had infected the entire project.

My colleague and I took a different approach. We held meetings and made sure people actually showed up to them. We asked questions before making demands; and we listened to what the teams had to say. We asked them for their opinions on the improvements needed before we presented our own suggestions. We didn't demand they implement every change immediately; we just asked them to think about it.

With each meeting, we emphasized that this was a group effort. We all had to work together to make the organization secure, and we were beside them every step of the way. We were making great strides together, and would keep improving over time. This wasn't a lie; we were moving in the right direction. The current situation was bad, but we kept this to ourselves, maintaining a positive, optimistic, and grateful approach to these team meetings.

The result: we got all the teams on our side. We got to compliance faster than expected and the teams even made improvements on their own, without our help.

And, we knew these changes would stick. Not only because we wrote a bunch of perfect policies that took into account every department's unique needs and priorities, but because we implemented robust and effective training programs.

Training programs are pivotal to long-term success, but they're almost as dreaded as a meeting with the resident downer, like Eli. Dry, checkbox-style training that everyone rushes through while answering emails on the second screen don't work. Real training connects to their daily work, showing them why the policy exists, what risk it reduces, and how it makes their job easier or safer.

And, like our meetings where we focused on the wins and improvements, training shouldn't revolve around fear or pointing out what people are doing wrong. Fear can force temporary compliance, but it kills long-term engagement. A culture built on punishment is a culture where employees hide mistakes, avoid reporting issues, and treat cybersecurity like an enemy. Instead, create an environment where security is a shared responsibility and success is recognized. Celebrate teams that follow policies well, share stories of prevented incidents, and make security part of everyday conversation—not just an annual training.

If you're someone who focuses on the negative, you're probably reading this with a lot of skepticism—but there's actually tons of research to back this up. Studies show that cybersecurity training is more effective when it's not built around fear, but around giving people agency, empowering them, and rewarding good behavior. People aren't robots. They respond to encouragement and optimism. And in cybersecurity, where we rely on others to act securely, that mindset is as valuable as any tool in our arsenal.

It isn't always simple to flip your attitude from negative to positive. Habits, fear of missing something, and the comfort of cynicism all get in the way. Security people worry that if they stop being critical, they'll overlook risks. Others fear embarrassment if they're seen as "too soft." And sometimes negativity is just habit, baked in over years of scanning for flaws. But just like everything else in this book, you absolutely have the power to shift your mindset here. Research in psychology calls this "learned optimism"—a skill you can train, not a personality trait you're born with.

One of the best ways to train optimism is the ABCDE model. It's simple to learn, but powerful when you actually use it.

- **Adversity.** Something goes wrong. A failed client call. A missed patch. A meeting that falls apart.
- **Belief**. Your brain jumps in with a story: "*They don't care. I'm bad at this. Nothing will change.*"
- **Consequence**. That belief drives your reaction. You withdraw. You criticize. You stop trying.
- **Disputation**. Here's the pivot. You fight the belief. Ask: *Is it always true? What evidence do I have?* Maybe the client was overwhelmed, not careless. Maybe you've solved harder problems before.
- **Energization**. The shift in belief creates energy. Instead of sulking, you lean in. You try again, this time with a different frame.

This isn't theory alone. It's grounded in cognitive-behavioral psychology, where challenging negative thoughts changes behavior (Seligman, 2011). Research shows people who practice disputation bounce back faster from setbacks and maintain motivation longer (Verywell Mind, 2024) .

There are plenty of books out there that go in-depth on how to be more positive; this isn't one of them. The subject is going to be a little different for everyone, so find the paths that resonate with you. This book is about cybersecurity—a field so often dominated by negativity. It just so happens that all that negativity is taking us nowhere fast. Instead, try bringing optimism to your next meeting; not only will this get you results, it'll help you stand out from the crowd—and keep people from hiding under their desks when they see you coming.

DAILY MICROPRACTICE

I am a positive and optimistic leader who sees opportunity in every challenge.

1. **Run the ABCDE check.**
   When you hit a setback, don't just stew. Write down: Adversity, Belief, Consequence, Disputation, Energization. Catch the thought, argue with it, flip the frame. One minute on paper can reset the whole spiral.

2. **Note one win.**
   At the end of every day, jot down a single security success—big or small. Someone reported a phishing email. A team patched faster than expected. That daily reminder trains your brain to look for progress, not just flaws.

3. **Say it out loud.**
   Spot a colleague doing security right? Call it out. In the meeting, in the chat, wherever. Recognition spreads. The more you celebrate wins, the more people repeat them.

ANALYTICAL

Reasons back to root causes without getting lost in irrelevant details

In 2012, Chris Anderson sat down with Elon Musk at SpaceX. Chris was impressed by, and curious about, the company's ability to reduce the price of the rockets.

"I tend to approach things from a physics framework," Elon said. "And physics teaches you to reason from first principles rather than by analogy. So I said, OK, let's look at the first principles. What is a rocket made of? Aerospace-grade aluminum alloys, plus some titanium, copper, and carbon fiber.

And then I asked, what is the value of those materials on the commodity market? It turned out that the materials cost of a rocket was around 2 percent of the typical price—which is a crazy ratio for a large mechanical product."

Elon Musk's *first-principle* thinking always returns to the root of an issue. That's the habit we need in security: strip issues to their essentials, reason from facts, and act on the smallest change that addresses the real cause.

"We need help," Alaina whispered while speed-walking over to Thomas and I at the security operations center. "Systems are down."

"Are you sure?" Thomas paled beside me.

"Yes," Alaina said, sitting down and opening her laptop. "Look."

The screen was filled with red crosses next to each system, indicating that they were down.

While Alaina and Thomas brainstormed at a fever-pitch, I pulled up the same page on my own screen, studying the rows of ominous red crosses.

"This could be two things," I started reasoning to myself. "Either all the systems are down, or the monitoring tools can't reach them. Option one is unlikely because if we were dealing with ransomware, the monitoring tool itself would also be down. In the case of option two, the monitoring tools need to use the network to reach the systems they are monitoring..."

I scanned the list, and one name caught my eye: "AMS-Firewall-Monitoring." This was the firewall located in Amsterdam that separated the IT monitoring tools from the rest of the network.

I clicked on the name and read the logs: "Certificate expired."

"Hey guys," I said out loud. "I know what the issue—"

"Shhh !" Thomas cut me off. "We restarted logging into all systems. We need to focus." "You're wasting your time," I said, a bit louder.

"Not now," Thomas snapped.

"Okay, then." I rolled my eyes, logged into the firewall, and renewed the certificate. Barely a minute later, all the alerts turned green and everything was up and running.

"What happened?" Alaina drew back, mouth hanging open in shock. "Everything is back up!"

"I tried telling you," I said with a shrug. "The certificate expired, so the network for the monitoring tool went down. The systems were fine, but the monitoring tool couldn't reach them."

Many IT or security professionals act just like my colleagues; they rush to conclusions without first reasoning back to the root cause. The excitement to use the latest AI tool ("maybe it can even solve the problem without me needing to figure out what the problem is!") overrides the need to slow down and think things through. From downed firewalls to new software, the tendency to overcorrect instead of using "first principle" thinking is a recurring theme.

If Alaina and Thomas had gone further on their own accord, they could have spent hours or even days trying to figure out the issue—wasting tons of time and losing trust.

This kind of thinking hurts us each and every time.

This doesn't just go for incidents; it also goes for security tooling. I see it all the time in our (in)ability to find good solutions for our security needs.

Instead of addressing the root of the issue, which often requires a small (and fairly cheap) fix, we rush to vendors to sell us the latest and greatest cybersecurity product. We waste time and money trying unvetted new tools instead of utilizing reliable, simple, and workable solutions.

And then, when that new software is lackluster or only does half the job for double the cost, it's on us to explain it to clients or bosses. I once dealt with a customer who wanted to audit logs from a critical application. He came to me with a list of all the vendors and solutions he found online. He couldn't figure out which one would be best, so he asked for my advice.

"Well, what specifically do you want to monitor, and why?" I asked.

"The board is concerned that administrators are making changes that aren't allowed," he said. "So we need to monitor that."

"Ah," I said. "So you want to keep track of the audit logs within the application. How often do you need to know? Do you need to know the minute a change is made, or is the board only concerned about potential long-term issues? What is the impact if you detect a change a week too late?"

"No impact at all," he said. "This only becomes an issue if someone is slowly stealing money, and that's a long-term risk. If they tried a big transfer all at once, we'd detect it anyway."

"Why don't you just check the application's audit logs once a week, then," I suggested. "Unless you need to do this for a lot of different applications or empty the treasury."

"Hmmm..." he thought through the idea, nodding. "Yeah, I think you're right. I don't know why we don't do that. But if we *did* need a new tool...""It's likely that none of these vendors can deliver what you need," I said. "They all talk about AI and amazing features, but I don't see where any of them would deal with the root of the problem. None of them say they'll send a message when there's a change in a custom application."

I let that sink in before continuing. "The funny part is that even if it has automatic detection features, you'd still need to log on and look at the same page you can manually check every week—for free!"

My client was thinking about all the different features of potential solutions, but he wasn't looking at the very basic need he was trying to fill: detecting a change in the audit logs. It's likely that he spent hours researching and reviewing these potential solutions, maybe even discussing them with others, when all he really had to do was spend some more time on the problem and the simplest requirements to solve it.

When you feel the pull towards assumptions, complexity, or vendor theater, follow these steps:

1) **Write the problem in observable facts.**
   Trigger + Impact + Evidence.

   "Monitoring shows all services down (evidence: SOC wall red). No user tickets. Started at 09:41 after firewall cert expiration warning."

2) **Generate two or three rival hypotheses.**
   Make sure you include at least one simple, boring cause. Ask, "What changed?"

3) **Design the fastest disconfirming test.**
   What would be true if this hypothesis holds? What's the 10-minute check? (E.g., test reachability from the monitoring network.)

4) **Apply the smallest effective fix.**
   Prefer a minimal change that resolves the cause (renew cert) over sweeping actions (rebuild hosts).

5) **Close the loop.**
   Record cause, fix, prevention (calendar cert reminder, monitoring for expiring certs), and the one sentence you'll need in the postmortem.

   If you find yourself stuck on any one of those steps, these questions will help:

   - Are we working on the wrong solution?
   - Are we trying to solve a problem that isn't a problem?
   - What, exactly, is the work that needs to be done?

Keep asking these questions until you've broken down the problem into its simplest form and found the root of the issue. Sometimes, office politics or bureaucracy limits your ability to ask those questions. If you can't question the problem or the project, at least ask yourself that third question: "What, exactly, is the work that needs to be done?"

I've found that many people fail to ask that specific question often enough, or don't work hard enough to truly answer it; which is a shame, because that one question solves most problems! Not reasoning from "first principles" results in huge lists of vague, unproductive work that fails to deliver meaningful improvements.

DAILY MICROPRACTICE

I reason back to the root of the problem.

1. **The "Why?" Factor**
   Pick one challenge you face today and ask "Why?" three times before reacting. Dig past the surface explanation until you find the root cause, even if it feels obvious. This simple habit trains you to see beyond distractions and focus on what truly matters.

2. **Write One Fact, Not a Story**
   Before tackling a task, write a single sentence describing the problem in observable terms. "The system stopped responding at 09:41." Not "The system is broken" or "The firewall failed." Training yourself to state facts cleanly keeps you from jumping to conclusions.

3. **Run the "Boring Hypothesis" Test**
   For every problem today, come up with at least one explanation that's dull and simple—expired cert, unplugged cable, wrong config. Test that first. Most issues really are boring, and proving it saves time, money, and stress.

METHODICAL

Maintains strong organization and structured thinking

It was a simple weekly status meeting, nothing fancy—just the usual routine to check progress, clear roadblocks, and keep everyone aligned.

We had barely gotten past the small talk about the weather when one teammate jumped in.

"I upgraded the firewall last week, and now I need support from the marketing department for the next stage," he said. So far, so good. But then: "The problem is, they don't listen..."

What started as a status update quickly became a five-minute rant about unresponsive stakeholders, ignored emails, and how "no one seems to care about security." The energy in the room shifted instantly—eyes dropped to laptops, people shuffled uncomfortably, and I could already see the meeting slipping away.

"Hold on a second," I cut in firmly but calmly. "Let's take this discussion to a separate meeting. This one's for quick status updates. If there's a deeper issue, we'll schedule time to resolve it properly."

He paused, nodded, and leaned back. The room relaxed. We moved on. Within ten minutes, everyone had shared their updates, flagged their roadblocks, and the meeting wrapped up on time.

Afterward, the manager came over.

"Thank you for keeping the structure. We would've been lost without that," he said.

I smiled. Moments like that remind me: structure is like oxygen. Without it, projects suffocate.

You see it all the time. Someone joins a conversation with the best of intentions, but then they start talking...and don't stop. One small detail turns into a long-winded story, which turns into a debate, which turns into chaos. By the end, no one remembers what the meeting was supposed to be about in the first place.

The consequences of a meeting spiraling off-track are bigger than most people realize:

- **Priorities become unclear**. People leave wondering what really matters and what to work on first.
- **Teams work on the wrong things.** Without clarity, energy gets poured into tasks that don't move the needle, and then even more time is spent fixing what went wrong—negative productivity.
- **Communication breaks down.** Important information gets lost, mixed with irrelevant noise.

One bad meeting doesn't just waste an hour; it can derail an entire week.

Being organized is more than just keeping notes and scheduling meetings; it's one of the clearest signs of leadership.

People notice when you can take a messy situation and bring clarity. Stakeholders see you as someone who is in control, someone they can trust. Executives, who already live in a world of back-to-back meetings and relentless decision-making, appreciate knowing that you've got everything in the information security department in line.

Organization keeps projects aligned and moving forward. Instead of drowning in distractions or running after ten different "priorities," a well-organized approach keeps everyone focused on what actually matters. It turns scattered conversations into clear actions.

And, it demonstrates professionalism. Decision-makers don't just want results; they want peace of mind. When you show up prepared, run efficient meetings, and keep everyone focused, you give them exactly that.

I follow a five-rule method for steering a project:

1. **Have a Simple Agenda and Stick to It**
   An agenda is a map. Without it, people wander and backtrack. Keep it short and visible to everyone, and stick to it like glue. If you're on a time crunch, put the duration for each topic and make it known that it's non-negotiable. A more thorough agenda template is available in the appendix, but an example agenda might look like:
   - Quick wins and accomplishments (5 mins)
   - Current roadblocks (10 mins)
   - Next steps and support needed (10 mins)

2. **Park Unrelated Topics**
   People often bring up real problems, but at the wrong time. Don't ignore them—acknowledge them and "park" them for follow-up: "That's a bigger discussion. I'm adding it to the parking lot so we can schedule a focused meeting just for it." This stops the derailment without dismissing valid concerns.

3. **Close Every Meeting with a Clear Summary and Next Steps**
   Never end with "Okay, I think we're done." That's how confusion creeps in. Instead:
   - Recap what was decided.
   - Assign who does what, and by when.
   - Confirm there are no outstanding questions

   This final minute prevents hours of "Wait, what are we supposed to do again?" emails.

4. **Be relentless**
   Be relentless in maintaining structure. Never end a meeting or a conversation without knowing exactly what needs to be done next and what the conclusion is. Sometimes, you have to hammer and repeat the question until you get what the information you need.

5. **Leave a paper trail**
   Write down what was decided. Write down what needs to happen next. Write down who owns what, and when it's due. Because here's the truth: if it's not written down, it didn't happen. Send out an email summarizing the meeting to all attendees and anyone not in attendance who needs to know. When things go wrong (and they will), people will ask, "Who decided this?" or "Why are we doing that?" If you don't have it in writing, you will spend hours digging through old emails. That's time you don't get back.

Being methodical should extend beyond meetings to every aspect of your workday. Documenting minor conversations by sending follow-up emails is good practice; it gives you power, showing that you know what's going on, and gives bosses, managers, and C-levels peace of mind that you have the details handled.

When you're writing policies, keep them understandable but thorough. A policy should tell the people reading it exactly what is expected, why it matters, and how they can succeed at following it. A *really* good policy will also include measurable, verifiable effects. If a policy cannot be checked, then it is little more than a suggestion. And suggestions, in cybersecurity, get ignored quickly.

Too often, I see policies that sound good but have no way to measure compliance. Take this one for example: "Ensure all critical systems are backed up." It sounds responsible, maybe even professional, but what does it mean in practice? Does "critical systems" mean production servers? Does "backed up" mean daily, weekly, monthly, or just when someone remembers? And how do you know if it's actually happening?

Instead, make it measurable: "Backup all production servers nightly, retain backups for 30 days, and test restores quarterly." Now you have something you can check. There's a clear schedule, a retention period, and a quality control step to verify that backups actually work.

This is important because when an incident happens, you don't want to argue about interpretation. You want to point to clear evidence that your policy is being followed—or know exactly where it is not. And when auditors or regulators come in, measurable policies make you look organized and credible.

Measurement also changes behavior. When people know there is a way to check compliance, they take the policy more seriously. It's human nature: what gets measured gets done.

So, when writing a policy, ask yourself one simple question: "How do we know if this is happening?" If you can't answer that with a clear process, a metric, or a check, rewrite the policy until you can. A policy without measurement is just wishful thinking dressed up in corporate language.

Even with things meant for your eyes only, being organized helps you maintain control over your projects. Keep your task list clean. Know what needs to be done today, what can wait until tomorrow, and what can be ignored altogether. Stay ahead of dependencies; know who you're waiting on and who's waiting on you.

It's not glamorous work, and it won't get applause in the moment. But weeks later, when a project is still on track and everyone knows what's going on, they'll notice. And they'll trust you more because of it.

And it doesn't stop there. Keeping structure also builds your personal reputation. People start to see you as someone who can bring order out of chaos. Someone who can take a room full of confusion and turn it into clear actions and direction. Over time, that reputation sticks. You become the person others trust when things feel uncertain, opening up more opportunities.

DAILY MICROPRACTICE

I am organized and maintain structure on my projects.

1. **Agenda and Summary Templates**
   Use the templates in Appendix B or build your own "plug and play" agenda and post-meeting recap that you can quickly tailor to every meeting.

2. **The "Parking Lot" Sentence**
   Practice one line until it rolls off your tongue: "That's important—let's park it for a separate session." Use it every time someone derails.

3. **One-Minute Wrap**
   Never leave a meeting without saying: "Quick recap—who's doing what, and by when?" It locks clarity in the room; follow up with a recap email within 24 hours.

RELIABLE

Manages projects effectively, maintains control, and delivers results.

He wanted another diagram.

For the third week in a row.

Weekly meetings with David, my client, followed the same pattern, over and over: small talk about the weather followed by 25 minutes spent discussing a new "visualization" of work I had already documented. And then David would ask for another visualization or a new diagram covering the same information we had just gone over. This time, he wanted an infrastructure diagram. Never mind that I had already provided this. Last week, it was a systems communication chart. Again, something I had already provided. Just like I had already provided a component status map.

It was driving me insane.

"Why does this keep happening?" I moaned as my colleague, Jack, sat down next to me. "He keeps asking for the same information we've already given him!"

"I have no idea," Jack sighed. "You've already explained and documented everything that there is to know."

That week, I decided that I wasn't going to waste my time. The diagram I'd provided already was good enough. I'd just explain it again.

The next meeting started as always.

"The weather is insanely nice today," David said, looking out the window with a smile

"Yeah, we got lucky," I agreed. "Last week it was horrible."

"I have a good feeling for this week." David folded his hands, eyes bright. "We're going to achieve something today."

I certainly hoped so.

"Before we dive into some of the progress we've made this past week, let's go over the drawing you requested."

I pulled up the diagram and explained it again—how the infrastructure worked, which systems would talk to other systems, the current progress of each and timeline for improvement, which systems were already implemented and which were going in next.

"You know what," David said, leaning back and studying the drawing. "I think we really need an infrastructure drawing that explains this better."

My jaw dropped. Jack coughed to hide a laugh.

"What do you mean by 'infrastructure diagram?'" I asked.

"I need to understand how the infrastructure works, which components talk to which," he replied.

"But that's what this diagram shows," I said, pointing on the screen to that exact information.

"No," he said. "I want an infrastructure diagram."

"This is an infrastructure diagram."

"Yeah, but not the infrastructure diagram I mean."

"Then what do you mean?"

"Something that explains the infrastructure," he said, voice beginning to rise. "We've been working on this diagram for months now," I said. "This diagram clearly explains the infrastructure."

"No," David said, slamming his fist on the table. "It doesn't. I need a REAL infrastructure diagram!"

I was so done with this. We needed to figure out what he wanted, here and now, no matter how rough the conversation got. "And what do you plan to do with a REAL infrastructure diagram?"

"I'm going to use it to know what's going on! I have no clue what we're doing." "That's what this does," I said, pointing to the diagram again. "And you know what? It's just a piece of paper. It won't change anything about the direction, scope, or work we're doing!"

"Please, let's take a short break," Jack said, trying to intervene as our conversation gradually got louder. His plea fell on deaf ears.

"Fine, if that's what you want," I said, grabbing a pen for the whiteboard. "Here you go."

I wrote quickly:

1. We finish setting up all the servers.
2. We connect all servers.
3. We harden the environment.
4. We are secure.

"There," I said. "Is that what you wanted?"

I threw the pen down; it slid to the middle of the table.

David didn't move, but his face softened as his eyes scanned the scrawled words on the whiteboard.

"Yeah," he mumbled. To me, the meeting could not have gone worse.

But, the next day, Jack walked up with a grin.

"I think you did it," he said.

"Did what?" I asked. Maybe he meant I got us fired; surely, the client hadn't come out of that meeting feeling good.

"You gave David what he wanted," Jack shrugged. "He just messaged me. Seems like it's all okay now."

"What do you mean?" I asked. "I lost my cool, just wrote down what we're planning to do like I was talking to a moron!"

"That's the thing," Jack said. "He seemed to think that you stayed calm and said EXACTLY what he wanted to hear."

"*That* is what he wanted to hear? Are you messing with me?"

"No," Jack said, chuckling. "That's all he wanted."

I couldn't believe it, then, but now I know exactly what was happening. The client needed the project broken down into clear, concise, user-friendly steps because my elaborate diagrams and drawings overwhelmed him. He thought he wanted more visualizations, but he actually needed less. He needed to know that his organization was in good hands, so he felt comfortable giving up control.

Clients don't usually ask for "a sense of control." Instead, they ask for documents, plans, diagrams, and drawings. Each time they ask, they express the need for another kind of document, and each time, they say something like, "Keep it short, to the point, do it quick." They don't want it to take time from the project.

Of course, they rarely understand how much time these diagrams and charts can take, and they certainly don't understand how unnecessary they are.

But they aren't actually asking for diagrams and visualizations. They're asking for control.

It's easy to fall into the trap of giving the client whatever they ask for, whenever they ask for it, but learning to say no is often one of the most important skills for a cybersecurity professional to have.

Don't give your clients the chance to exert endless bids for control. Accommodating these requests gives them license to get in the way, step on your tail, and waste your time. The more you present them with information and drawings that they don't really understand, the more insecure they become. They start asking colleagues for support, trying to intervene, and setting up extra unnecessary calls. You wind up feeling micromanaged, and the project gets delayed as you spend more time soothing their nerves and performing unnecessary, ancillary tasks than getting the job done.

That doesn't mean you shouldn't try to make the client feel confident in the project; it's that you need to make them feel confident in you. And you can do that by being a great project manager, showing results, and proving that someone is steering the ship.

That someone is *you.*

When we talk about project management as it relates to cyber projects, we're talking about a more complex, coordinated, and—to many people—confusing process than a typical technology implementation. Project management in cyber requires many different departments and people, covering a more invasive set of changes and standards.

For example, if you need to comply with any a standard like the ISO27001 , you don't just need to change a few things; you need to change many different components of the organization, from the way HR recruits people and stores personal information to technical improvements to the website run by marketing. Some improvements are related to the process, some are technical, some are cultural, and some are governance; it's a whole complex mesh of different topics and expertise. Cyber projects require a different kind of mentality to normal projects. Agile project management techniques like SCRUM won't work here. The more waterfall-based project management techniques like Prince2 can become too complex and, because of all the different stakeholders involved, also hard to plan out.

So, what should you do instead?

Instead of applying the same project management technique on each project, you need to focus on what technique will best fit each scenario. Smaller projects could work better with small increments, such as weekly or bi-weekly status meetings. Others are more complicated and might benefit from a more waterfall-based approach to get the stakeholders on board. In the most complex projects, many stakeholders can't work with you if you don't have a strong predefined planning, because cybersecurity changes are on top of their day-to-day work. They need to see accurate timelines to make sure your plans fit into theirs.

However, no matter which method or combination of methods you are trying to use, you need to have some visualizations in your toolbox. One of the most powerful you can use is still the Gantt chart. If you immediately rolled your eyes reading that, you're not alone; many security experts dread using the Gantt chart . Yes, it's boring and time-consuming to make—but it's also one of the most versatile and effective ways to convey your project management plan to your client.

Only the Gantt chart can show the planning and complexity you need in cybersecurity projects. It also lets you think as much as you need to about stakeholder dependence and the flow of tasks.

In addition, the Gantt chart is a tool for showcasing the future to stakeholders. And since most stakeholders don't understand every aspect of the topics involved in a cybersecurity project, you need the Gantt chart to show them what is going on and what kind of work needs to be done. Without the Gantt chart, most stakeholders have no clue.

And when they don't know, they become nervous. They want to see you are in control, and they want to feel like they have some control over the process. Just knowing when things will be happening, when other stakeholders need to be called for, and what each change will lead to, can give them that sense of control they're so desperate for.

Keep in mind that a good project manager isn't measured by how many things go right; they're also measured in how many things go wrong without completely derailing the timeline. Projects rarely ever move in straight lines. They zig, they stall, they sometimes crash face-first into a wall. That's normal.

What matters isn't whether problems happen—it's how you respond when they do.

When setbacks hit, your job is to keep the steering wheel steady. Don't panic, overexplain, or drown your stakeholders in excuses. Instead:

1. **Name the issue.** Use clear, simple language and avoid catastrophizing or complicating things.
2. **Show the fix.** Updated plan, new dates, new owners.
3. **Reframe the progress.** Remind them what's already done so they don't spiral into thinking the whole ship's sinking.

People don't freak out because of problems. They freak out because they think no one's in control. Show them you're in control—even when the system fails—and they'll stay calm.

A few rules I live by:

- Be realistic with timelines. Cybersecurity work always uncovers surprises. Bake in buffer.
- Match detail to the audience. Executives want bullet points; engineers want specifics. Give each group only what they can use.
- Never overpromise. "We'll try" beats "We'll definitely deliver" when you're not sure. Clients respect honesty more than fairy tales.

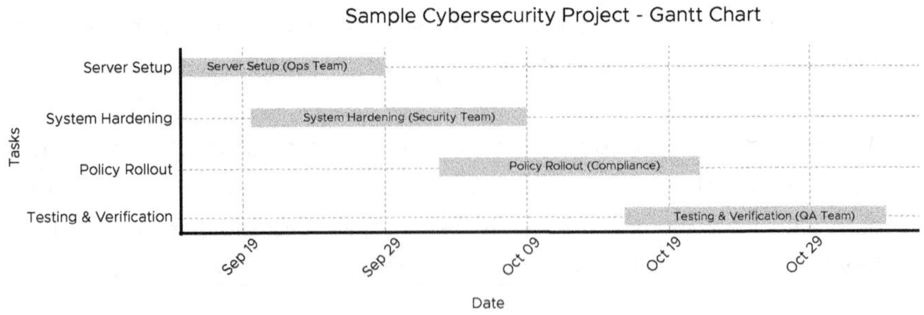

Being "reliable" doesn't mean bending to every client request or smiling while you're drowning in busywork. It means steering projects through complexity, setbacks, and doubt—while proving that someone is at the helm. That's what clients actually buy. Not the diagram. Not the chart. You.

And when they ask for "control"? You give them confidence instead.

DAILY MICROPRACTICE

I am efficient and reliable, and others trust me to take control.

1. **Anchor Every Update in Outcomes**
   Instead of rattling off tasks completed, tie each update to what it means for their business goal. They don't just hear "done"; they hear "value delivered." That reframes you as a partner, not a vendor.

2. **Keep a "One-Pager" Ready**
   Instead of cranking out new diagrams, keep a single one-pager that shows scope, timeline, and current status. Update it weekly. Share it at every touchpoint. Cuts noise, builds confidence.

3. **Run a Weekly "Red Flag Check"**
   Every Friday, scan for risks: delays, missing input, shifting priorities. Call them out before the client does. When they see you spotting problems early, they trust you when chaos hits.

BOLD

Dares to make decisions and act with conviction.

Something was off at FreshRoute Logistics. I had been brought on as an external consultant, and in the three weeks I'd been in the office, I'd noticed that this seemingly straightforward company was undercut by anxiety and pressure.

Things came to a head one afternoon. It was a normal day: keyboards tapping, coffee brewing, phones ringing. But I overheard a conversation across the aisle, between two employees.

Mike—sharp-eyed, deliberate, the sort who rewrote drafts even of Slack messages—leaned in toward Sara. His voice was deliberately low.

"It's like James doesn't even care," he muttered. "FreshRoute is walking blindfolded into disaster. Their network security's a joke, and he's not listening. It's almost like he's hiding something."

Sara frowned, twisting a bright curl around one finger, eyes darting sideways. "You're right," she murmured, too fast. "We've handed him a solid strategy, but he's stonewalling. There's got to be something else at play here."

They slid into jargon—"TLS 1.2 deprecation," "syslog aggregation," "key rotation." But the urgency in their cadence showed that these weren't technical debates. They were strategizing.

Eventually, their footsteps faded toward the server room.

At first, I'd treated my role as I always did; I was a neutral observer, and my job was to make sure that the tech team and the execs stayed on the same page. But I, like Mike and Sara, was concerned about what I'd seen.

FreshRoute's infrastructure was flimsy—patchwork systems masking operational entropy. Yet requests for security improvements were delayed, minimized, redirected. Why?

People whispered about an external audit, and a hush fell whenever the CFO passed. James, the IT lead, looked overwhelmed and disheartened. So, instead of jumping into the consulting part of my consulting role, I found myself feeling like a spy. I was putting together clues: interrupted Teams threads, erased whiteboard, a VPN server with mismatched logs.

Was Mike right? Was James hiding something?

Just then, my phone buzzed. *James Foster*.

"Hey," he said, skipping the usual small talk. His voice was strained. "Got five minutes?"

I did; but we'd need a lot more than five minutes.

"James, let's get real. What's your *actual* top priority here? What needs locking down—today?"

He hesitated. "We're growing faster than we planned for. We're improvising infrastructure, patching as we go. It's—it's risky."

He cleared his throat. "One breach and we're done. Deliveries halted. Client contracts voided. Even our transport licenses... We can't afford that. Not now."

His voice sounded panicked now. "We've been looking at AI-based monitoring, behavioral baselines, full encryption sweeps—"

"James." I cut in sharply. "Forget the buzzwords. What's the *actual* critical exposure?"

There was a pause. I could feel the pivot in the silence.

"User accounts," he admitted. "New hires, temporary drivers, reused passwords... We've seen strange logins. I think someone's poking us. Quietly."

"And the data?"

"Route intel. Delivery schedules. We're holding sensitive data for high-profile clients. If that leaks..." He didn't finish the thought.

Now we were getting somewhere. No more evasion. No more panicked distractions.

"Then we start with accounts," I said. "Identity is everything. You can't secure what you can't authenticate."

James exhaled, the tension in his voice dipping slightly. "I know," he said, more to himself than me. "But it's complicated."

"Why?" I asked flatly.

"Because Lisa wants to see ROI, not risks," he said bitterly. "And Mark wants flashy AI dashboards and machine learning. Something he can talk about on investor calls."

"And the auditors?"

"They've started using phrases like 'systemic weakness.' That's never good." It became clear: James wasn't just fighting an invisible threat outside the firewall—he was caught in a storm of internal politics.

Lisa, the CFO, wanted to trim fat. No appetite for proactive spending.

Mark, the CEO, chased innovation theater. "Shiny object syndrome," I'd call it elsewhere. Here, it was fatal.

The auditors? An ambiguous threat, setting up plausible deniability in case it all burned down.

So I drew a line.

"Here's what we do," I said. "We document one bold, irrefutable move. Something so clearly necessary, so unambiguously responsible, that it creates a paper trail no one can dispute."

"Lisa won't like it," James said, chewing his lip.

"She'll like an exposure incident even less."

James nodded, slowly.

"Alright," he said. "We harden authentication. Account audits. Strong policies, MFA rollout. Password resets across the board. Clean house."

"Good," I said.

"But—" His voice caught. "If this gets pushback, I may need backup. If Mark or Lisa start calling it fear-mongering..."

"You won't be alone," I said, careful to sound more certain than I felt.

"Let's do it," he said, a cautious relief in his voice.

We hung up, but the discomfort lingered.

The vulnerability wasn't just digital. It was layered in people—their pride, their pressure, their politics.

I tapped my pen against a pad. James had known all along what needed to be done; why hadn't he put his foot down and done it? Was he hoping that, somehow, he could make everyone happy?

Of course, standing up to your bosses and clients isn't always easy. It takes conviction—courage. When you know what's best for your organization, but everyone is standing against you, it can feel like you're one hobbit facing down an army of orcs.

But trying everything isn't bravery — it's the opposite.

The single biggest reason an information security project fails is that we aren't making informed, confident, bold decisions. Instead, we try to do a bit of everything, and in this confusion, we talk past each other, waste time trying the same thing twice, overlook the big picture getting hung up on details, and fumble through half-baked ideas.

It's especially difficult when you've got executives asking for things that you know won't work, or assigning a budget that won't be enough. It can feel like the easiest thing to do is say "yes" to them, while also finding some way to do the thing you *know* will work.

When you try a dozen things, you can only afford to spend a fraction of the time it probably requires to make one of them work. And each time you have to start over, you're saying: "this didn't work, this didn't work, this didn't work." That's a lot of negativity to present to stakeholders, making us seem confused, ineffective, insecure and negative.

I'm sure that, right now, you're asking: "But what if I'm wrong about my one big, bold idea? What if I spend all this time and resources on something that doesn't work? Meanwhile, my client is relying on me!"

Your client will feel better hearing "this didn't work" once than over and over, even if it took more time to get to that "this didn't work." And they'll definitely feel better when their data is secure because you stood your ground rather than giving in to their ideas or adhering to an unrealistic budget.

Give yourself credit for your expertise; if you think you have the solution, and can make a good case for it, then trust yourself. Failing with one idea, if you pursue it fully, will almost surely reveal new information that can help you make the next solution a win.

Be confident, not nervous or apologetic, when you approach your client with a solution, especially if it clashes with their expectations. Most business executives won't follow the logic behind a technical project; they just want to hear that you know what you're talking about. And, if that idea fails, be confident when you explain why. Mention what the failure taught you, and how it showed you a better solution.

But what if a client still won't budge? I've been in a few of those situations myself, where the client insisted on doing the work a certain way—even if I explained why another method would be better. Now, when that happens, I lay out all the different options, tell them which I recommend, and give them three reasons why *their* preferred solution won't work as well—if it works at all. If they still insist, I tell them: "I'm willing to do it that way, as long as you understand the risks and potential inefficiencies. Do you still want me to go ahead?"

And then, I do the work (even if it doesn't work). This way, I can stand firm in my conviction that it's the wrong way to go without betraying the customer's right to choose for themselves. If you give your client all the information they need to make the choice—including challenging their status quo—and they make the wrong one, that's not on you. Sometimes, clients just have to see for themselves that their approach was wrong.

The pride and enjoyment you take at work is also a consideration. We cybersecurity experts enjoy diving deep into a project rather than scattering our attention in many directions. Coming up with daring, creative solutions will make you happier at work—and that will make you more capable and devoted to the cause.

So, let's say that you know you're not making brave, bold choices at work. You leave decision-making to others, you let others direct your attention to whatever they think is right, you don't commit to a few approaches to cybersecurity but try everything simultaneously, leading to a lot of half-baked projects. Your calendar is constantly filled with meetings because you don't have the courage to say "no" to things you know won't work or are a waste of your time.

Now you know your dragon; but how do you even begin to slay it?

As with most of these characteristics, the key is to start small. Paradoxically, since being bold can often be about making big moves, you want to figure out where you can repeatedly make a small impact without going too far out of your comfort zone. Go far enough to keep yourself on your toes, but not so far that you can't recover if something goes wrong.

Start by being braver about small things. Start each morning by making one bold decision about your day. One of my personal bravery practices is to write out the important tasks on the docket for the day—tasks which are important, and which, if left unfulfilled, will disappoint someone.

Then, I go through the list and cross out some of those tasks (sometimes as many as ten or twenty!). The tasks I crossed out will *not* get done that day; even if that leaves someone angry or disappointed.

Choosing what to exclude is a bold decision; you need to trust in your judgement that you are excluding the right things. If and when I second-guess myself, I remind myself of the characteristics of a good security expert. I remember that I need to be bold and make decisions.

This is just one small practice to make yourself more bold and more decisive.

Once you notice you are naturally starting to make bolder decisions, you can also become braver in conversations with stakeholders. Say no more than is strictly necessary, be confident and direct, point out flaws in their argument or gaps in their knowledge, and come up with strong actions, excluding everything else. This, of course, also requires diplomacy and perceptiveness; you never want to alienate people by being rude. Be patient, listen well, but still stand firm in your choices—often, that's the only way to get real work done.

DAILY MICROPRACTICE

I am bold and decisive; I speak my mind and commit to things even when others disagree.

1. **Cross It Out**
   Each morning, write down your task list. Then deliberately cross out one to three tasks you will not do today. Commit to letting them go. This forces you to make a call, prioritize, and deal with the fallout of saying "no."

2. **One Hard "No" a Day**
   Every day, pick one moment where you say "no" to something you know is a waste of your time or energy—whether it's a meeting, a low-value task, or a shiny but useless request. Do it politely, but firmly.

3. **Stake a Claim in Conversations**
   In one meeting or conversation each day, voice your clear stance on

ADAPTABLE

Adjusts easily to new roles and organizational cultures.

It was common knowledge around the office that Daan was one of our best security engineers. Any client would be lucky to have him as their consultant—especially a smaller customer like Hi-Res. Hi-Res had bought a security solution four years prior, but they weren't happy with it.

We all thought that Daan had it covered. And, from a technical standpoint, he did. He knew how to fix and improve systems, and within a week of taking on the assignment, solutions were in place; a week later and the system was running better than ever. In two weeks, Daan did something Hi-Res had been trying to do for years.

Now, he was ready to take the system to the next level, transforming it into a security powerhouse. If he could connect some logs, the system's threat-detection capabilities would be supercharged. But this step required the client's help, and cooperation from several internal departments within the client's organization.

He waited, and he waited, and he waited for the pieces to fall into place at Hi-Res.

But the earliest meeting he could get with the client was a month out.

So he tried a workaround. In a meeting with one of the other departments at Hi-Res, he asked if they could configure the system from their end, making it possible for him to start work on the improvements immediately. They agreed—but when Daan asked, two weeks later, they said they hadn't gotten around to it.

"We might get to it next month," said the department head.

Daan could not, and would not wait a month. So, he started on another project to improve the system. Again, this required input from another Hi-Res team.

"Sure," the team leader said during the meeting. "We'll do it next week."

"Maybe next month," the team leader said two weeks later when Daan followed up.

Now Daan was getting frustrated, and decided to bring his complaints to the client.

"That's how it goes here," Hi-Res said. "You have to be patient."

So, Daan resolved to be patient and move at the clients' speed. In the meantime, he would improve parts of the system that didn't require any input from other departments.

A year later, Daan handed the Hi-Res project over to me.

"They're a pain," he told me, clearly frustrated. "They're impossible to work with. They're so slow, they never deliver on time, so you can't get anything done."

That piqued my curiosity. When I spoke to the client, they had similar things to say about Daan. Given Daan's well-deserved reputation for security expertise, this was a shock. But the customer described how many of the systems' essential functions weren't working. Simply put, Hi-Res wasn't getting what they wanted from the system.

I realized that neither Daan nor the customer was wrong. The system would work much better if the organization had done everything Daan wanted them to do, when he wanted them to do it. But, Daan should have seen that his approach wasn't working, and the result only hurt the client.

And, in the end, it was Daan's job to make sure the client was secure—even if it meant adapting his approach.

Daan had thought he was slowing down to match Hi-Res' pace, but even that was still much faster than they were ever going to move. So I shifted my timelines to months, not weeks. I set up multiple meetings anytime I needed a department to accomplish something, since I knew my first request would go undone. And, I made the system simpler, because the customer needed to be able to use the system even if someone on some team wasn't playing their part in some new improvement or update.

Sure, simplifying the system meant that Hi-Res wasn't as secure and resilient as they *could* have been if all the upgrades were implemented immediately—but not having a functional system at all would be way worse.

And, I found, that because the system was easier to navigate, employees at Hi-Res started to use the security system themselves. They would perform their own security analyses, and ask questions that allowed me to step back from day-to-day operations and focus on the things that would make a bigger difference in the long run.

Daan was brilliant, but he was trying to play chess with checkers pieces. He wanted precision, speed, and cutting-edge improvements, while the customer wanted slow, reliable, predictable change.

They simply weren't a good fit.

That's why being able to *make* yourself a good fit for any client is a pivotal part of being a good security expert. My work on Hi-Res' system didn't make me a better engineer than Daan; but knowing how to match the organization's culture helped me keep them safer.

Each company is different. Different cultures, different kinds of people, different processes—you name it, each is different in its own way. In cyber, we tend to see the same threats over and over: ransomware, phishing, viruses. This might be true, but treating each organization as though it has the same threat *profile* is a mistake.

Every organization is vulnerable in its own unique ways and, thus, needs different strategies. For instance, at a software company you might sell security for its own sake; they want to produce high-quality tech and security is a crucial part of that. But a medical office of doctors and nurses might be deaf to an IT expert's suggestions to learn a new protocol because they've already studied for years; the last thing they want to do now is more learning in a completely different subject.

Some organizations thrive on speed. They move fast, break things, fix them, and keep running. For them, being slow kills trust—they expect you to act like them: fast, agile, decisive.

Others are political. They run on relationships, consensus, and carefully managed change. Push too fast and you'll trigger resistance so strong it'll undo all your work. With them, you have to move slower, build alliances, and get everyone nodding before even touching the system.

Adapting yourself and your strategies to the environment you're in is part of being an efficient and effective cybersecurity expert. When you meet with resistance, keep your complaints to yourself and instead ask: where's the friction coming from? What am I doing that's not working with the way this organization is run? How can I remove some of these roadblocks and make sure they get the security they need?

It might be a matter of changing your approach—slowing down or simplifying, like I did for Hi-Res. Try to empathize with the people on the other side of the screen or desk. What does their workload look like, and how does what you need fit into (or create conflict with) that? Imagine the way they work best and adapt your role to effectively fit into their day.

It might also be time to turn your focus back to values. If you see that the resistance is coming from a lack of urgency on the organization's part, you might revisit the question of what the client cares about. How can you get stakeholder's on the side of strong cybersecurity? What argument would convince them to play ball?

Whenever you walk into a new organization, stop and read the room. Ask yourself:

- Is this a culture of speed or stability?
- Do decisions flow top-down or through layers of politics?
- What pace will make them comfortable enough actually to adopt change?

Then adapt your style to fit. Sometimes that means moving fast. Sometimes that means slowing way down. Either way, the goal is the same: get security done in a way that sticks.

Apply the same approach when you're writing policies. I get it. There are thousands of free templates online—whole libraries of policies that look professional, full of impressive words like "governance" and "data stewardship." It's tempting to grab one, change the logo, and call it done. But copying someone else's policy—assuming that what worked for one company will work for all companies—is one of the easiest mistakes I see cybersecurity professionals make.

Policies aren't wallpaper. They are instructions, rules that tell teams how to act when something goes wrong. And if those rules don't match how the organization actually works, they fail before they're even published.

A tech giant might have policies that cover multiple data centers spread across continents, entire teams dedicated just to key management, and budgets that dwarf a smaller company's annual revenue. If you copy their encryption policy word-for-word, you'll probably find yourself telling a one-person IT team to build something impossible. That's not security; it's chaos.

Instead, do the work to write a bespoke policy for your organization, taking into considerations their specific risks, people, culture, and business goals. If the client handles sensitive customer information, focus on protecting that information in ways the team can realistically implement and maintain. If the company prides itself on speed and flexibility, then write policies that guide secure decision-making without turning every change request into a ten-step approval nightmare. On the other hand, if they're in a regulated industry where compliance is non-negotiable, your policies need to show that level of rigor.

And, be adaptive when it comes to the industry as a whole. Policies are not stone tablets handed down from the mountain. They are living documents, meant to shift and flex as your environment does. Cybersecurity changes at a pace that leaves most heads spinning. New threats emerge daily, new technologies roll out weekly, and regulatory bodies seem to release new requirements every quarter. If your policies stay the same while everything else moves, you're already behind.

That's why policies must be reviewed regularly. At the very least, do it annually. But don't wait for a scheduled review if something major happens—a merger, a new regulation, a critical incident, or the adoption of a new core technology. The point of a policy isn't to look good in an audit; it's to keep the organization safe now.

And don't lock yourself into rigid technical choices that will age badly. This is especially true if you're a consultant who won't be there for years to monitor.

If your policy still mentions “DES encryption” because it sounded cutting-edge when it was written, that’s a failure waiting to happen. Instead, focus on intent and adaptability: “Encrypt all data at rest using the latest recommendation by NIST.” That one sentence keeps you secure today and tomorrow, no matter how encryption evolves.

Policies become part of a business’ DNA. Get them wrong, and you inject confusion. Get them right, and they make the organization stronger.

Remember that our role is more important than a business’ bottom line: there are real people behind those numbers, employees and customers alike, who can get caught in the crossfire when threats become attacks. Most people aren’t going to become your friend, and some may even frustrate or annoy you, but they still deserve to have their personal data and income protected from attacks. Daan wasn’t able to make his workflow and Hi-Res’ culture align, and perhaps there’s nothing he could have done to change that outcome; but you can most certainly work on becoming more flexible and adaptive, so that you’re more helpful to more organizations and make the world safer and more secure.

DAILY MICROPRACTICE

I am adaptable and align with company culture to get the job done.

1. **See it from Their Perspective**
   Identify a part of your organization's culture that is at odds with your personality or preferences. Instead of getting frustrated, think about how this aspect has its benefits and how you can use it to your advantage in making the business more secure.

2. **Design for Imperfection**
   Stop expecting every team to deliver flawlessly. Build systems and policies that still function even if one department drags its feet. Simpler, resilient solutions beat fragile "perfect" ones that collapse without full cooperation.

3. **Write for the Reality, Not the Template**
   When drafting policies, don't copy-paste a big tech giant's governance docs. Walk the halls. Learn the workflows, values, and constraints of this organization. Then write short, actionable rules they can actually follow. For more about writing solid policies, see Appendix B.

CONCLUSION

I used to believe that technical skill was everything. If I knew how to configure firewalls better, if I understood every endpoint, if I could run circles around SIEM queries and penetration tests, I would be untouchable. That was the picture I had in my head of what made a great cybersecurity expert.

That belief fueled me for months as I worked on a machine learning based detection system, refining every line of code, tuning every alert. It was perfect—or so I thought. The day I finally presented it to a manager, I expected excitement, gratitude, maybe even admiration. Instead, they nodded politely and moved on to the next agenda item. No questions. No action. Nothing changed.

That moment stung. I had given them something powerful, something that could stop an attacker in their tracks, and it landed with all the impact of a dull spreadsheet. I remember thinking: My work doesn't matter

It wasn't the technology. It wasn't even the results. It was me. I hadn't connected the dots between what I built and what they cared about. I had built something to stop hackers, but they needed something to protect their revenue, their reputation, their ability to do business tomorrow. I hadn't spoken their language.

That was the moment I realized technical skill wasn't enough. It's still important, but without communication, influence, and alignment, it's just noise.

This book exists because of that moment. I don't want anyone else to feel that same hollow silence after delivering something powerful. It's for every cybersecurity expert who knows they can do more—if only they can shift how they think, how they work, and how they lead.

When I started writing this book, I thought about where most of us begin in cybersecurity: tools, alerts, and long nights hunched over dashboards trying to catch the next threat before it catches us. We start with firewalls, antivirus logs, phishing simulations—the things we can see, touch, and configure. And for many of us, that's the whole game for a long time: build defenses, respond to incidents, repeat.

But that's not where we ended up, is it?

We started with the old picture of a cybersecurity expert—technical, reactive, often isolated—and we ended with someone very different: someone who leads, communicates with clarity, aligns security with business goals, and makes bold decisions even when things are uncertain. Someone who doesn't just guard the gates but helps steer the entire direction of the organization.

The shift is subtle at first. You don't throw away your technical knowledge; you build on it. You learn to frame risk in ways people care about, to make tough decisions that cut through noise, to focus on value. And when you do, you find yourself not just reacting to threats but shaping how your organization sees them, responds to them, and even uses them as a chance to grow.

The characteristics in this book weren't chosen at random. They came from real work, real mistakes, and real successes—the kind you only learn after being thrown into complex situations where technical answers aren't enough. The threats we face today move faster, hit harder, and often exploit weaknesses that have nothing to do with outdated software or missing patches. They exploit people. They exploit organizations that can't make decisions quickly enough, that can't get everyone aligned, that fail to communicate what matters.

That's why these characteristics are about mindset as much as skill. Being brave enough to make bold decisions. Understanding how value is created, not just how systems are secured. Communicating in ways people understand. Staying positive, forward-thinking, and focused on solutions rather than problems.

They're not just professional "nice-to-haves." They're survival skills.

Think of it this way: if technical skill is the engine, these characteristics are the steering wheel. Without them, you're moving fast but don't know where you're going—or worse, you're heading straight for a wall. But with them, you're not just moving, you're navigating. You're making choices that create trust, buy-in, and real change.

And the best part? They're learnable. No one is born with perfect communication skills or fearless decision-making. These are traits you build, step by step, until they become habits. This book was designed to help you do exactly that—because the difference between a good cybersecurity professional and a great one is often just a handful of habits applied consistently.

Mindset is what turns knowledge into influence. You can be the smartest person in the room, but if your mindset is fixed on proving yourself right instead of solving problems together, people will tune you out.

I learned this the hard way. Early in my career, I thought the best way to earn respect was to be correct. I'd walk into meetings loaded with data, ready to counter every objection with facts and frameworks. And yet, instead of winning people over, I often walked out frustrated, wondering why no one acted on my advice.

What I didn't understand back then was this: influence isn't about winning arguments. It's about changing perspectives creating clarity where there is confusion, showing a path forward that feels possible rather than overwhelming.

That requires a very different mindset. One that values listening as much as speaking. One that sees resistance not as a challenge to your authority, but as an opportunity to understand what truly matters to the other person. One that focuses on outcomes instead of ego.

When you adopt this mindset, everything changes. People start to come to you, not because you have the "right" answer, but because you make it easier for them to move forward. They see you as a partner, not just a security gatekeeper. Once people trust you, your ability to influence grows exponentially.

That's why I spent so much time in this book on how to think, not just what to do. Because the mindset you carry into every conversation, every project, every difficult decision—that's what determines whether your work becomes shelfware or lasting change.

Now it's your turn.

Reading this book is a start, but change doesn't happen because you read words on a page—it happens because you act. And that starts small. You don't need to overhaul your entire approach to security overnight. You just need to take one step.

Pick one characteristic from this book that feels the most uncomfortable. The one you'd rather avoid. That discomfort is a signal—it's where the real growth is hiding. Maybe it's being brave enough to make a decision without endless consensus. Maybe it's communicating clearly instead of hiding behind jargon. Maybe it's slowing down long enough to understand what your stakeholders actually value.

Whatever it is, start there. Today.

Take one bold action you wouldn't have taken yesterday. Speak up in that meeting where you'd normally stay quiet. Reframe a technical recommendation in terms of business outcomes instead of system uptime. Decide what not to do today so you can focus on what matters most.

If there's one thing I want you to take from this book, it's this: your mindset is the multiplier. It amplifies every skill, every hour of work, every technical certification you earn. When you align that mindset with action, you stop being just another person solving security problems; you become someone shaping how the entire organization sees them.

The future of cybersecurity is not something to fear—it's something to look forward to. Yes, the threats are growing. Yes, technology is advancing faster than ever. But that also means the opportunities for those who can adapt, influence, and lead are greater than they have ever been.

We are moving into a world where cybersecurity professionals are no longer hidden behind ticket queues and incident dashboards. Instead, they are at the table when the biggest decisions are made: shaping products, influencing strategies, and even driving revenue by building trust into everything the organization delivers.

Think about that for a moment. Not too long ago, most security teams were seen as blockers. Now, the best security teams are business enablers. They create safer digital experiences, protect customer trust, and reduce risk in ways that directly impact growth. And the professionals who rise in this environment are the ones who combine their technical knowledge with the mindset, communication, and leadership skills we've talked about throughout this book.

This is why optimism matters. If you approach security with fear of failure, fear of making the wrong decision, or fear of not knowing enough, you'll hold yourself back. But when you approach it with curiosity and confidence, when you see every challenge as a chance to learn and every obstacle as a chance to influence, you unlock a completely different future for yourself and your organization.

The landscape will continue to shift, but you now have the tools to shift with it. You have the ability to lead, to adapt, and to drive meaningful change. And that's something worth being excited about.

APPENDIX A: TOOLS TO DRIVE VALUE

As we've seen, modern cybersecurity demands more than just technical expertise—it requires clarity, structure, and a direct link to business goals. Too often, security strategies collapse under their own complexity or lose relevance because they fail to connect to what actually drives an organization forward.

Even with a complete mindset overhaul, you still need an external framework for applying your new business skills in real-world situations where they can make a difference.

As a consultant, I regularly make use of two practical tools to address that gap: the **Risk Model Canvas** and the **Cybersecurity Canvas**.

- The **Risk Model Canvas** helps map business processes, identify critical assets, and link them directly to security risks. Instead of generic checklists or abstract threat catalogs, it frames risk in terms of business impact, making security decisions easier to justify and prioritize.

- The **Cybersecurity Canvas** takes that one step further by aligning my security initiatives with the organization's larger goals and needs. It ensures cybersecurity is not an isolated IT project but an integrated part of the company's growth, reputation, and operational resilience.

These tools give you a visual, straightforward way to engage stakeholders, highlight what matters most, and ensure that your cybersecurity approach protects not just technology—but the business.

RISK MODEL CANVAS = BUSINESS MODEL CANVAS + RISK

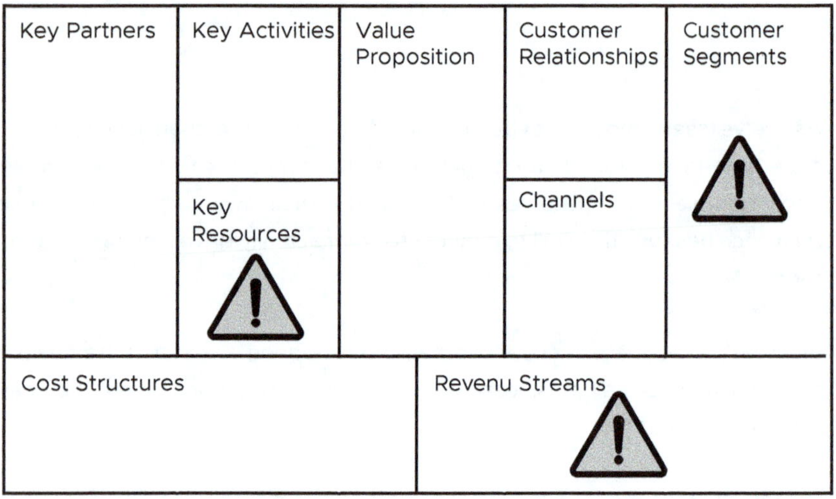

Risk Model Canvas is based on the Business Model Canvas by Strategyzer

SAAS Company

Key Partners

Operational
Finance Administration
Recruitment Agencies
Investors
Marketing Partner

IT infrastructure
Hosting
Cloude provider
Data suppliers
Software library
Supplier
Software mode
supplier

Knowledge
Industry Netwerok &
alliance
Knowledge partner

Key Activities

Product Development
(Design, Build, Test, Maintain)

Product delivery
(Configure, test, release, maintain)

Customer Support
(Support, Gather, Analyze & Report on data

Sales & Marketing

Key Resources

Developers
Designers
All other employees
(Sales, HRM, finance, customer support)
Owners, shareholders

Code base (IP)

Production data

Value Proposition

Software as a Service

White label/Own label

Customer Relationships

Trust and communication

Channels

Website & app

Direct trageted marketing

brokers

Customer Segments

Companies in need of the platform

Cost Structures

Cost Structures

70% Human resource relates costs

30% Other costs (Housing, Data and Telecom costs and Cloud, Marketing, PR & Advertising, and Travel costs

Revenu Streams

Recurring Revenu 80%

Custom Development 20%

Whenever I get a new client, my first step is to learn everything I can about them and map out their Business Model Canvas. The Business Model Canvas covers nine essential blocks: Customer Segments, Value Propositions, Channels, Customer Relationships, Revenue Streams, Key Resources, Key Activities, Key Partners, and Cost Structure.

When I took on Forthrite, the retailer who was won over by our ability to secure their app, I immediately did a deep dive into their website.

First, I considered their **Customer Segments**. As the name suggests, that's their primary customer base. Forthrite targeted fashion-forward individuals who prefer the convenience of mobile shopping—primarily web-native millennials and Gen Z users who are never far from their phones.

Next, the **Value Propositions**. I had to find out what value the company offered to their customers or clients. My client offered trendy clothing at affordable prices, all accessible through an easy-to-use app. Their unique selling point was the seamless shopping experience combined with exclusive app-only deals.

Then, the **Channels** they use—where most of their sales or profit-generating business took place. Their primary channel was the mobile app, but they also leveraged social media platforms for marketing and customer engagement.

For **Customer Relationships**, I looked at how they maintained a loyal customer base beyond one-off buyers. Their focus was on personalized interactions through app notifications, responsive customer service, and loyalty programs that keep users coming back.

Moving on to **Revenue Streams**, a category that speaks for itself. Their income was generated from direct sales within the app with additional revenue from premium features or advertising partnerships.

Their **Key Resources**, or the most critical assets for day-to-day and overall operations, were their mobile app, their physical inventory, brand reputation, and data they collected on customer preferences.

The **Key Activities**, which can be thought of as the primary workflow of the employees that kept the business running, included app development and maintenance, inventory management, marketing campaigns, and providing excellent customer service.

As for **Key Partners**, or other stakeholders outside the business that played into their success, they collaborated with clothing manufacturers, app developers, payment processors, and influencers for marketing purposes.

Finally, the **Cost Structure**. How much did it cost to run the business, and which costs were most critical versus which had the greatest return in profits? Major expenses for Forthrite involved app development and maintenance costs, marketing expenditures, supply chain logistics, and operational costs like staffing and customer service.

By filling out each block, the bigger picture became clear: the app was the heartbeat of their business.

I took out a red pen and started circling out all their digital components with potential risks.

Any security breach to the app wouldn't just be a technical issue; it would strike at the core of their value proposition and revenue streams.

With Business Model Canvas, I aligned our cybersecurity efforts directly with their business model. It wasn't just about checking boxes, but safeguarding what truly matters to them.

For cybersecurity purposes, the next evolution of the Business Model Canvas is the Risk Model Canvas—that's where we connect threats and vulnerabilities to the business model.

A week later, during our meeting with the client, I presented the canvas directly to the CTO and asked for his feedback on what situations made him feel uneasy regarding cybersecurity threats. He mentioned, obviously, that the app itself going down could be disastrous; there was also the payment traffic through the app and the potential for theft. He also brought up data breaches and the large amount of customer information they handled. A leak would hurt their reputation.

Using that as a baseline, we continued through the Risk Model Canvas together.

Customer Segments: "Do any customer requirements pose potential compliance risks?""Yes," the CTO replied. "Especially with international customers. We need to comply with GDPR and other regional data protection laws."

Value Propositions: "What threats could undermine the unique benefits you offer?"
He sighed. "If our app becomes unreliable or if exclusive deals leak before they're announced, it could diminish our competitive edge."

Channels: "Are there legal issues that could interfere with how you reach customers?"

"Definitely," he said. "Privacy laws impact how we use push notifications and email marketing. We have to be careful not to violate any regulations."

Customer Relationships: "Are there risks in how you manage customer interactions?"

He nodded. "If our customer service platform is compromised, it could lead to unauthorized access to customer accounts."

Key Resources: "What if a critical resource becomes unavailable?"

"If our app goes down, even for an hour, we lose significant revenue. Our infrastructure needs to be highly reliable."

Key Partners: "Do any partners have access to sensitive data?"

"Yes," he admitted. "Our cloud service providers and some third-party developers do. We're concerned about their security measures."

Key Activities: "What happens if an essential activity is disrupted?"

"If our supply chain is interrupted, we can't fulfill orders, which directly impacts customer satisfaction and revenue."

Revenue Streams: "Could a security breach affect your financial stability?"

"Absolutely," he said. "Any loss of customer trust would result in decreased sales. Plus, we might face fines for non-compliance."

Cost Structure: "Are there risks associated with your major expenses?"

He considered this. "If our app development costs spike due to emergency fixes from security breaches, it could strain our budget."

By the end of our discussion, we had a comprehensive list of potential risks, directly informed by the CTO's insights aligned with the business model. And, he was impressed with the time we'd taken to understand his business. It made a big difference in how good he felt about bringing us on, and made him much more open to working with our suggestions and budgetary needs. He greenlit our plan of action because we weren't just external consultants anymore—we were partners invested in their success.

Cybersecurity is there to help organizations and businesses stay alive. In the end, what matters most is that businesses can keep on making money and reach their goals. And information security is, whether we like it or not, a supporting factor in that whole ordeal. To us, as experts and professionals information security is the star of the show, the sun around which everything else revolves.

But to our clients, it's only a supporting factor—and part of our job is to make sure it doesn't get relegated to a bit player. Like it or not, the modern cyber professional needs to be able to understand the business side of the business, not just the technical side.

Just like you need to know your assets before you can start protecting them, you first have to know the business before you can protect it the right way. The Risk Model Canvas shows the client that you're paying attention to the whole picture, and helps you tailor your approach to bring the most value and earn the most support.

CYBERSECURITY CANVAS

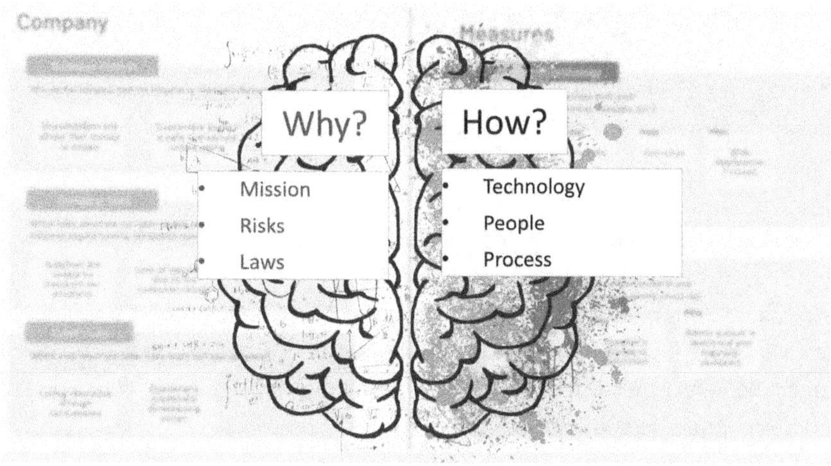

I've seen it too many times. A company panics, throws money at cybersecurity, and thinks they're safe. Spoiler: they're not.

The first mistake? Random tool purchases.

Some shiny new AI-driven endpoint detection with all the buzzwords? They buy it. A firewall with "military-grade" encryption? Add it to the cart. No clear reason why. No strategy. Just noise.

The second mistake? Overly technical focus.

They geek out over tools and forget what actually keeps the business alive. It's like fortifying the castle walls while leaving the treasury door wide open because "we installed the latest patch." Security doesn't live in a vacuum—it has to connect to the business.

And the third? Treating security as an IT problem.

As if only the IT guys care if the company gets breached. Cybersecurity is everyone's problem. Finance, sales, HR—they all bleed when things go wrong. But many strategies still sit buried in the server room, divorced from what really matters: the business itself.

I consulted a company that made this exact mistake. They threw a small fortune at tools: endpoint protection, DLP, a shiny SIEM, even an overpriced threat intel feed. Looked impressive on paper. But no one asked why. No one tied security to business goals or customer trust.

Six months later, a new C-level person came in. He looked at the budget and said, "Cut it all."

He didn't see value—because there wasn't any communicated value.
All those tools? Gone. All that work? Wasted.

The company ended up weaker than before because their "strategy" was just tech without purpose.

That's why most cybersecurity strategies fail. They confuse action with direction.

A thousand controls don't matter if you're protecting the wrong things.

That's when I realized I needed to find a new approach to demonstrating value to the customer. And that's where the Cybersecurity Canvas comes in. "The Cybersecurity Canvas," I said. "One page. All your security priorities in one place. Simple enough to explain to your board, strong enough to guide your next five moves."

It's not a checklist, or a framework that takes months to decode. It's a visual map—a way to line up cybersecurity with what actually keeps your business alive.

Security is often chaos. Too many tools, too many threats, too many opinions. The Canvas cuts through the noise:

- Simplicity – no one gets lost in a 100-page policy doc.
- Focus – you see exactly what matters most, fast.
- Buy-in – leadership actually gets it. And when they get it, they back it.

Think of the Risk Model Canvas as the map of your customer's business risks. Now think of the Cybersecurity Canvas as the playbook for protecting it. One tells you what's at stake, the other tells you how you fight back.

BREAKING DOWN THE CYBERSECURITY CANVAS

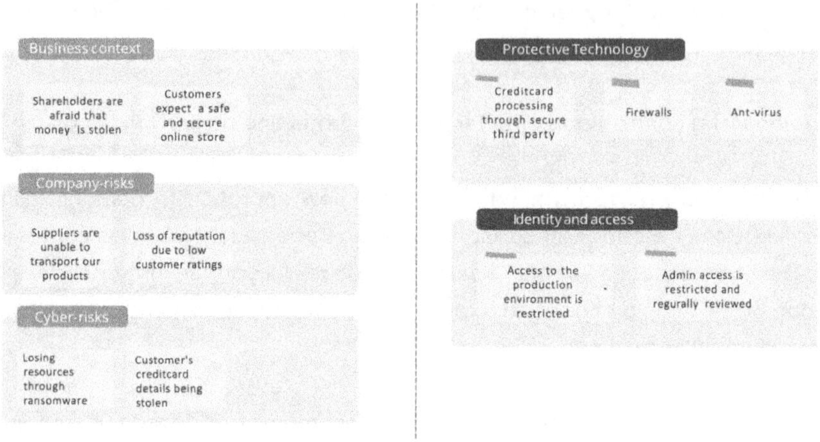

The Cybersecurity Canvas works like a brain. It has a left side and a right side. The left side is about logical thinking—figure out what your business drivers are and the related risks. If you've already completed the Risk Model Canvas, this should be easy to fill in.

The right side is the creative side, where you come with creative solutions to tackle the risks of the left side.

LEFT SIDE – WHY CYBERSECURITY MATTERS

The left side of the Cybersecurity Canvas is about context. It's where you map out why cybersecurity matters in the first place.

Business Context (or Business Drivers)

Start with what drives the business. Is it revenue from digital sales? Protecting a strong brand reputation? Meeting strict compliance demands? Maintaining customer trust? These are not "nice-to-have" goals; they are the reasons the business exists. Every security effort needs to tie back to one or more of these drivers. If it doesn't, it's noise.

Risk Landscape

Next, identify what could disrupt those drivers. Are ransomware attacks likely to paralyze operations? Could phishing campaigns expose sensitive data? Is insider risk something to watch? Your threat landscape should reflect realistic dangers based on the type of business you're protecting—not generic threats copied from a report. This part is about knowing what really could go wrong.

Compliance Requirements

Finally, map out the rules that shape how security needs to be implemented. Laws like GDPR, CCPA, or PCI-DSS can dictate what data you must protect and how you handle it. Non-compliance doesn't just bring fines; it erodes trust and can halt business operations entirely.

RIGHT SIDE – HOW WE FIGHT BACK

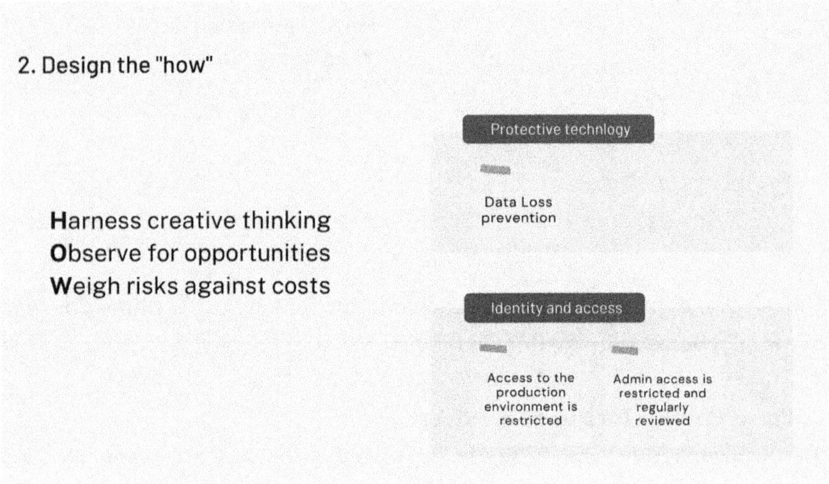

This side is about action. This side is about **how** we are going to tackle cybersecurity problems. It's where strategy becomes real, and theory turns into measures that actually reduce risk.

Every company has its own landscape, its own crown jewels, and its own ways to fail, so the right side changes depending on the context. Every company tends to have its own right side; yes, there might be some similarities, but details always differ.

Designing the right side of the Cybersecurity Canvas requires some level of creativity. There's no one-size-fits-all solution to every individual company's individual risk landscape. You need to be able to tailor solutions to your client, and that takes bold, creative strategies. It's tempting to just use an existing framework, like the ISO27001 or NIST. These are safe choices; we can't be sure of the results of any given strategy, and it's hard to measure how much security efforts are actually going, so existing frameworks feel like a safety net.

But it rarely works, because it lacks prioritization and a connection to the actual risks of the organization. Rather than designing an individualized program that targets actual business needs and threats, it creates a lot of noise and insufficient protection of key areas.

The Cybersecurity Canvas allows you the freedom to design it yourself, choosing your own components and individual controls within those components to fit the risks you want to tackle.

For example, if you have a business continuity risk, and you develop a software, it might be good to use some DDOS protection as a protective control against the most common DDOS attacks that could bring your business down. We could categorize this control under "Protective Technology" as is done in the basic version of the Cybersecurity Canvas. However, you are not beholden to this approach. You can decide that another category fits better, like "Business Continuity" or a certain ISO27001/2 chapter that you want to highlight.

Design the right side however you see fit, in whatever way makes sense for your client.

For small companies, you can generally divide your program into three distinct boxes:

- Protective Technology
- Identity & Access
- Awareness & Training

My latest research into cybersecurity and small businesses shows that these are the three most important arenas to focus on.

What goes inside the categories is different for every company. Some companies develop software, some manage large supply chains. It's up to you to figure out which controls are important and will actively help protect the business.

For example, a retail company that sells clothing online may depend on a website developed by a third party for the majority of their sales. In that case, it might be beneficial to add a control to check and validate the website every few months if it still meets the expected security standards.

That said, you aren't beholden to these categories alone, or at all. I have seen people use the Cybersecurity Canvas differently, such as adding a category for the ISO27001 as their basic set of controls then adding another box for "focused effort" for the controls that directly tackle areas of risk that went beyond the scope of the ISO27001. Make the Cybersecurity Canvas work for you, so you can make it work for your client.

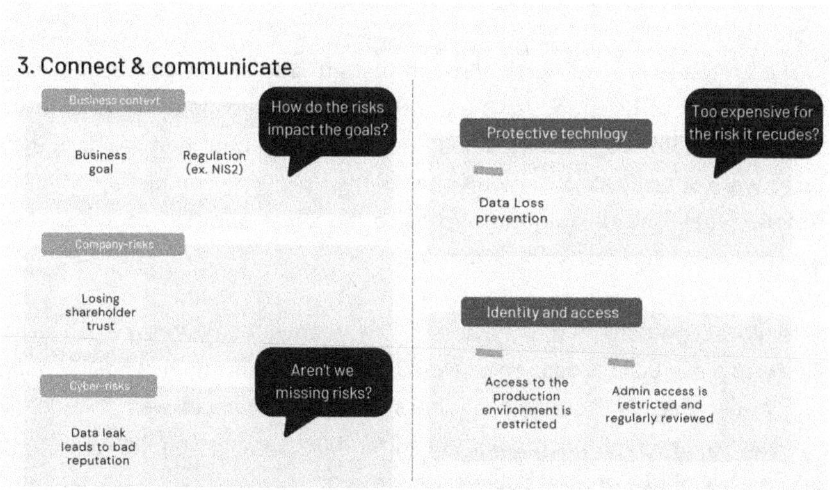

When I ask business leaders what keeps them up at night or what kinds of breaches are likely to ruin their company, I often get silence—or something like, "We have antivirus, so we're okay, right?"

That's where the two sides of the brain become powerful. It forces you to connect the dots: What actions, processes, or technologies will reduce those risks most effectively?

The Cybersecurity Canvas is a one-pager, so you can easily print it on, share it in a slide and fill it in together. And then keep asking: What are the dots and how are they connected? Did we cover everything on the left side? What components are we missing? Do we have controls on the right side that don't connect to the left side? Should we stop doing those things?

The most effective use of the Cybersecurity Canvas I've ever seen was during two sessions I did for four healthcare companies. These healthcare companies were direct competitors and colleagues; each had exactly (or almost exactly) the same business model.

In the first sessions, we went through the left side of the canvas. Tackling the context, the risks and laws and regulations. Interestingly enough, even though the companies seemed near-identical, only about half the risks they faces were actually alike. The other half of the risks were completely different because they had unique approaches to the same business process, each with its own weaknesses and strengths.

After collecting data on the first session. I went to work and drew 3 canvases. One was a minimal canvas, which would cost the organization almost nothing but would lead to increased business risks. One canvas was completely risk-averse, at a high price point but with robust security in place. The third occupied a middle ground between those two.

In the second session, I laid out the three canvases. That's when the magic happened. For the first time, every leader in the room—from operations to finance to IT—was speaking the same language. They weren't talking about "firewalls" or "patches"; they were talking about business risk, trade-offs, and value. The COO challenged a control's cost. The CFO asked how it tied to revenue protection. The CTO weighed resilience against complexity. Suddenly, cybersecurity wasn't buried in IT—it was a boardroom conversation.

In the end, that's what the Cybersecurity Canvas brings to the table. It forces you to slow down, strip out the noise, and connect security to what actually matters. Not tools for tools' sake. Not fear-driven spending. Not another 100-page policy no one reads. Just a clear map that shows the business why security matters and how to protect it.

Leaders stop nodding politely and start debating trade-offs, weighing costs, and owning decisions. The Canvas turns vague "IT talk" into real business strategy. It gives every stakeholder the same language, the same picture, and the same focus.

And that's the difference. Without it, security stays scattered—just another list of controls no one understands. With it, security becomes sharp, focused, and tied directly to the lifeblood of the business. The Cybersecurity Canvas doesn't just make security simpler—it makes it matter.

APPENDIX B: TOOLS TO DRIVE COMMUNICATION

I hope this book has demonstrated that technical mastery alone doesn't guarantee influence, and influence is a primary factor for success in information security. You can be the smartest person in the room and still lose the argument if you can't communicate strategically or give stakeholders confidence that you're in control. Many security professionals stumble not because they lack expertise, but because they struggle to translate that expertise into language and interactions that win trust.

Shifting from "expert" to "persuader" requires practice. It's about reading people as well as reading code, shaping conversations as well as systems, and knowing when to pivot in the moment. These aren't skills most of us were trained in, but they're often the difference between being heard and being dismissed.

To help bridge that gap, this section of the appendix collects practical tools for building communication and business skills. You'll find frameworks for reading the room, pivoting when a meeting goes sideways, reinforcing positive behaviors, and structuring your interactions with clients through agendas and follow-up emails.

Together, these resources give you concrete ways to move beyond "being right" and toward being effective—ensuring your voice carries weight not just because of what you know, but because of how you deliver it.

These sections are by no means exhaustive. They only scratch the surface. If you really want to level up your communication, check out courses or books that go deeper.

PERCEPTIVE SKILLS: BODY LANGUAGE CHEAT SHEET

Want to learn to be more perceptive? This cheat sheet can help you spot nonverbal cues that reveal how clients or stakeholders are really feeling (beyond what's coming out of their mouths).

Engagement Signals

Leaning in → Interest, agreement, engagement

Nods → Encouragement, approval, following along

Open palms → Honesty, receptiveness

Note-taking → Valuing information, buy-in

Disengagement Signals

Leaning back, crossed arms → Resistance, defensiveness

Glancing at phone or watch → Boredom, impatience

Lack of eye contact → Discomfort, distraction, low confidence

Slouched posture → Low energy, disengagement

Agreement / Alignment

Mirroring your posture or gestures → Rapport, alignment

Quick smiles or chuckles → Agreement, trust

Leaning toward materials/slides → Curiosity, interest

Resistance / Discomfort

Tight lips or jaw → Tension, holding back disagreement

Rapid blinking → Stress, cognitive overload

Arms crossed with legs angled away → Closed off, distancing

Side glances at peers → Looking for backup, silent dissent

Power & Influence Cues

Others look toward them before answering → Informal authority

Upright posture, expansive gestures → Confidence, dominance

Interrupting often → Asserting control, sometimes insecurity

Minimal movement, poker face → Deliberate neutrality (often decision-makers)

QUICK PIVOT MOVES

When you notice negative signals:

- **Disengagement:** Ask an open question — "What's most useful for you here?"
- **Resistance**: Acknowledge and redirect — "I hear some concerns. Let's talk about them before moving on."
- **Power cue**: Engage them directly (find out what they value) — "How does this fit with your priorities?"

PERCEPTIVE SKILLS: "READING THE ROOM" MEETING WORKSHEET

Remember, meetings are a lot more complex than just who's technically right. Use this quick scan to assess group dynamics, spot hidden resistance, and stay flexible. Bring one copy to every client meeting. Keep your notes short and factual — just enough to spot patterns across multiple meetings.

1. Energy Scan (first 60 seconds)
   ☐ Overall mood: ☐ Positive ☐ Neutral ☐ Tense ☐ Distracted
   ☐ Who is leaning in? ____________________
   ☐ Who is leaning back/closed off? ____________________
   ☐ Who avoids eye contact? ____________________

2. Influence Map (ongoing)
   ☐ Who speaks first? ____________________
   ☐ Who do others look to before responding? ____________________
   ☐ Who stays quiet but reacts strongly? ____________________

3. Micro-Checks (5 minutes in)
   When you pause and ask, "How does this land with you?" or "What am I missing?":
   ☐ Who responds quickly? ____________________
   ☐ Who hesitates or deflects? ____________________
   ☐ Any side glances or subtle signals? ____________________

4. Tempo Adjustment (throughout)
   - ☐ Should I slow down and ask more questions? ____________
   - ☐ Should I move faster to match engagement? ____________
   - ☐ Did my pace shift the mood? ____________

5. Debrief (after meeting)
   - ☐ Who seemed most resistant? ____________
   - ☐ Who supported me without prompting? ____________
   - ☐ What shifted the mood today? ____________
   - ☐ Whose values do I already align with? ____________
   - ☐ What values do I need to align with? ____________

PERCEPTIVE AND PERSUASIVE SKILLS: THE PIVOT PLAYBOOK

When you sense resistance or disengagement, don't push harder on the same track. Use this framework to shift your tactics mid-meeting without losing credibility. You can also use the worksheet provided during meetings to keep you on track and review afterwards to see what did or didn't work.

Step 1. Notice the Signal

Signs of disengagement: phones out, short answers, crossed arms, sighs.
Signs of confusion: long pauses, repeated questions, glazed eyes.
Signs of resistance: tension in tone, side conversations, "yes, but..." replies.

Step 2. Diagnose Quickly

Ask yourself: Is this a content problem (they don't get it), a framing problem (they don't buy it), or an emotional problem (they don't feel heard)?

Step 3. Choose Your Pivot Tactic

Content problem (they don't get it) → Simplify. Reframe in plain language, give an example, or draw a quick diagram. Find a way to establish yourself as being in control of the project even if they don't "get it".
Framing problem → Re-anchor in value. Shift from technical detail to business outcome: "Here's what this means for revenue/efficiency."
Emotional problem → Pause and listen. Ask a neutral check-in question: "What's top of mind for you right now?"

Step 4. Reset the Room

Name the pivot explicitly and steer forward:

"Let's zoom out for a moment..."

"I think the real question here is how this ties back to your top priority..."

"Sounds like I need to clarify X before we move on."

Step 5. Capture the Win

When the mood shifts, don't gloss over it. Acknowledge the turn:

"This was a good reset — I appreciate the pushback."

This makes the pivot feel intentional rather than like you lost ground.

WORKSHEET: PIVOT IN REAL TIME

1. **Spot the Signal**
   - ☐ Disengagement (phones out, silence, body language)
   - ☐ Confusion (questions repeat, blank stares)
   - ☐ Resistance ("yes, but...," tense tone)

2. **Diagnose**
   - ☐ Content (they don't get it)
   - ☐ Framing (they don't buy it)
   - ☐ Emotional (they don't feel heard)

3. **Pivot Choice**
   - ☐ Simplify (plain words, example, visual, establish sense of control)
   - ☐ Re-anchor in value (link to business outcomes)
   - ☐ Pause + listen (neutral check-in)

4. **Reset Statement (circle one or write your own):**

   "Let's zoom out..."

   "The real question here is..."

   "Let me clarify before we move on."

5. **After the Meeting**
   - ☐ Did the pivot work? Y/N
   - ☐ What tactic unlocked progress? ______________________
   - ☐ What would I try differently next time? ________________

OPTIMISTIC SKILLS: POSITIVITY IN CYBERSECURITY TRAINING

Replace fear-based messaging with constructive, confidence-building language that motivates employees to adopt good security habits. Employees engage more when they feel like they help create and protect value, not like you see them as liabilities or programs to troubleshoot. Use this template during training prep or live when you catch yourself slipping into pessimism. You can even use it as a group exercise; Ask participants to reframe one pessimistic example into a positive statement. You'll reinforce the lesson and make the language theirs.

Step 1. Start With the Negative Statement (Pessimism)

"Don't click suspicious links — you'll get us hacked."

Step 2. Identify the Desired Behavior

- ☐ Reporting suspicious emails
- ☐ Locking devices
- ☐ Using strong passwords
- ☐ Updating software
- ☐ Other:____

Step 3. Apply the Reframe Formula

Instead of:

"Don't [negative behavior] — [fearful consequence]."

Say:

"When you [positive behavior], it [beneficial outcome]."

Step 4. Fill in the Blanks

When you ______________________________,

it ______________________________

Examples:

When you report a suspicious email, it protects the entire team.

When you update your software, it keeps our systems fast and reliable.

When you use a strong password, it safeguards customer trust.

Step 5. Practice (Try It Yourself)

Pessimistic: "If you leave your laptop unlocked, someone could steal data."

- ❑ Optimistic: When you ____________, it ______________________.

  Pessimistic: "If you use weak passwords, hackers will get in."

- ❑ Optimistic: When you ____________, it ______________________.

  Pessimistic: "If you don't report phishing, we could lose millions."

- ❑ Optimistic: When you ____________, it ______________________.

METHODICAL SKILLS:
MEETING AGENDA AND POST-MEETING RECAP TEMPLATES

Keep meetings focused, signal control, and reassure clients you're steering. Meeting agendas can be shared in advance or printed and distributed at the meeting; you should send the recap within 24 hours. This demonstrates that you're reliable and methodical, reduces misunderstandings, and builds confidence in your leadership.

Subject line: Agenda – [Project/Topic] Meeting – [Date]

Header:

Project: ______________________________

Date/Time: ______________________________

Participants: ______________________________

Agenda:

1. **Welcome / Objective (2 min)**
   - Why we're here today.
2. **Updates (5–10 min)**
   - Progress since last meeting.
   - Key metrics/status.
3. **Discussion Items (15–20 min)**
   - [Topic 1]
   - [Topic 2]
   - [Topic 3]
4. **Risks & Decisions (10 min)**
   - Any red flags to resolve.
   - Decisions required today.
5. **Next Steps (5 min)**
   - Who owns what, by when.
   - Confirm date of next meeting.

Notes:

- Keep agenda short.
- Attach your one-pager/status sheet if relevant.

Subject line: Recap & Next Steps – [Project/Topic] – [Date]

Body:

Hi [Names],

Thanks for your time today. Here's a quick recap:

Key Outcomes:

– [Decision/Agreement 1]
– [Decision/Agreement 2]

Next Steps:

– [Person A] will [task] by [date].
– [Person B] will [task] by [date].
– [You/Your team] will [task] by [date].

Risks/Watch Items:

– [Risk/Issue 1]
– [Risk/Issue 2]

Please reply if I've missed or misrepresented anything. Otherwise, we'll proceed as outlined.

Best,
[Your Name]

ANALYTICAL SKILLS: ROOT-CAUSE THINKING

Cut through noise, avoid wasted effort, and solve problems at their source instead of piling on complexity or reaching for the latest AI tool. Don't just record what went wrong; record the simplest check that could have spotted it sooner.

Step 1. Write the Problem in Facts

Trigger + Impact + Evidence

- Trigger: ______________________________
- Impact: ______________________________
- Evidence: ______________________________

(Example: Monitoring shows all services down. No user tickets. Started 09:41 after firewall cert expiration warning.)

Step 2. Generate Rival Hypotheses

☐ Hypothesis 1 (likely cause): ____________________

☐ Hypothesis 2 (alternative): ____________________

☐ Hypothesis 3 (boring/simple cause): ____________________

Step 3. Design the Fastest Disconfirming Test

What would be true if each hypothesis holds?

☐ Test for H1: ______________________________

☐ Test for H2: ______________________________

☐ Test for H3: ______________________________

(Aim for a 10-minute check, not a two-day rebuild.)

Step 4. Apply the Smallest Effective Fix

☐ Minimal fix: ______________________________

☐Avoid overreaction: ____________________

Step 5. Close the Loop

- ☐ Root cause confirmed: ____________________
- ☐Fix applied: ____________________
- ☐ Prevention step (reminder, automation, doc): ____________________
- ☐ Postmortem one-liner: ____________________

POLICY WRITING FRAMEWORK

Create security policies that people will actually follow. Instead of copy-paste templates, use this framework to draft policies that fit your organization's size, culture, and risks.

Step 1. Define the "Why"

- ☐ What risk or behavior does this policy address?
- ☐ Why does it matter to this organization (speed, compliance, customer trust, uptime)?

Step 2. Match the Culture

- ☐ How do decisions really get made here (top-down, consensus, speed-first)?
- ☐ What tone and level of detail will people accept and follow?

Step 3. Write for Action

- ☐ One sentence per rule, written in plain language.
- ☐ Use "must" for non-negotiable requirements; use "should" for guidance.
- ☐ Avoid technical jargon that will age badly ("DES encryption") — use intent-based language ("Encrypt all data at rest using latest NIST recommendations").

Step 4. Keep It Practical

- ☐ Are responsibilities clear? (Who does what, by when, using what tools?)
- ☐ Is the policy realistic for the team's actual resources and skills?
- ☐ Could a new hire follow it on day one?

Step 5. Build for Change

- ☐ When will this policy be reviewed? (Annual at minimum, or after major incidents/regulatory changes.)
- ☐ Does it allow flexibility as tech and threats evolve?

Quick Policy Checklist

Before publishing, ask:

- ☐ Does this policy solve a real problem?
- ☐ Does it reflect how the organization actually works?
- ☐ Is it simple enough to be followed without training wheels?
- ☐ Does it tell people what to do in a crisis?
- ☐ Does it stand the test of time (intent over rigid detail)?

www.ingramcontent.com/pod-product-compliance
Lightning Source LLC
LaVergne TN
LVHW050822061126
851857LV00012B/928